Emil Selenka

A zoological pocket-book:

Or, Synopsis of animal classification. Comprising definitions of the Phyla, classes,

and orders, with explanatory remarks and tables

Emil Selenka

A zoological pocket-book:
Or, Synopsis of animal classification. Comprising definitions of the Phyla, classes, and orders, with explanatory remarks and tables

ISBN/EAN: 9783337815172

Printed in Europe, USA, Canada, Australia, Japan

Cover: Foto ©ninafisch / pixelio.de

More available books at **www.hansebooks.com**

A ZOOLOGICAL POCKET-BOOK:

OR,

SYNOPSIS OF ANIMAL CLASSIFICATION.

COMPRISING DEFINITIONS OF THE PHYLA, CLASSES, AND ORDERS, WITH EXPLANATORY REMARKS AND TABLES.

BY

Dr EMIL SELENKA,

PROFESSOR OF ZOOLOGY IN THE UNIVERSITY OF ERLANGEN.

TRANSLATED FROM THE THIRD GERMAN EDITION

BY

J. R. AINSWORTH DAVIS, B.A.,

TRIN. COLL. CAMB.

LECTURER ON BIOLOGY AND GEOLOGY, UNIVERSITY COLLEGE, ABERYSTWYTH; AUTHOR OF
"A TEXT-BOOK OF BIOLOGY," ETC.

Interleaved for Students' Notes.

LONDON:
CHARLES GRIFFIN AND COMPANY.
EXETER STREET, STRAND.
1890.

TABLE OF CONTENTS.

A

Grade A.   **PROTOZOA** (Plastidozoa).

Unicellular organisms.   The cell-body (sarcode, protoplasm) effects the reception and assimilation of food; the endoplast or nucleus (chromatin and nucleolus; nuclear fluid) plays an important part in reproduction.   One or more contractile vacuoles frequently present.   Reproduction effected by fission, gemmation, or spore-formation (often after preceding conjugation or copulation).

All Protozoans live in water, damp places, or as parasites in the juices of other animals.

Class I. **Rhizopoda** (Gymnomyxa).

Protozoans devoid of cuticle whose protoplasmic body takes in food, and, in many cases, moves by means of retractile pseudopodia. A skeleton frequently present. Reproduction by fission or formation of swarm-spores.

Order 1. *Proteomyxa.* A heterogeneous group of small forms with inconspicuous nuclei, and pseudopodia of various nature : **Protomyxa, Protomonas, Vampyrella, Protogenes, Archerina.**

Order 2. *Labyrinthulidea.* Protozoans consisting of a protoplasmic network with travelling spindles : **Labyrinthula, Chlamydomyxa.**

Order 3. *Mycetozoa* (Myxomycetes). Rhizopods in which the body is an active plasmodium, producing coated spores : **Ceratium, Trichia, Æthalium** (flowers of tan).

Order 4. *Amœboidea.* Shape-changing Rhizopods with a contractile vacuole. Movement and reception of food effected by means of blunt pseudopodia. Sometimes a skeleton. Reproduction usually by binary fission, sometimes by gemmation. Resting-cysts (hypnocysts) common— **Amœba, Lithamœba, Hyalodiscus, Plakopus, Pelomyxa, Difflugia** with membranous shell strengthened by foreign particles, **Arcella** with shagreen-like shell.

Order 5. *Foraminifera* (Reticularia). Rhizopods with an amœba-like body, emitting filiform pseudopodia which branch and anastomose. Possess a (usually calcareous) shell.

A. I m p e r f o r a t a. Shell with a single or a sieve-like opening; (more rarely two or a few openings).—**Gromia**, one-chambered. **Miliolina**, many-chambered.

B. P e r f o r a t a. Shell with pores. **Lagena. Orbulina; Globigerina. Polystomella; Nummulina. Eozoön, a** doubtful form from the Precambrian (Laurentian).

Order 6. *Heliozoa.* Globular Rhizopods, with fine stiff radiating pseudopodia. Protoplasm containing one or more nuclei and contractile vacuoles, and very numerous non-contractile vacuoles. A siliceous skeleton sometimes present. Cyst- and spore-formation may take place. **Actinosphærium** and **Actinophrys sol,** sun animalcule, without skeleton. **Raphidiophrys,** with loose tangential spicules. **Acanthocystis,** with radial spicules. **Clathrulina,** stalked, and with perforated spherical shell. Lead on to

Order 7. *Radiolaria.* Marine Rhizopods of globular or conical shape, with differentiated protoplasmic body. Radiating filamentous pseudopodia, central nucleus-containing capsule, and (generally) a radial or tangential skeleton of silica or acanthin. No contractile vacuole. Reproduction by fission or swarm-spores. Parasitic (?) or symbiotic (?) yellow corpuscles very generally present. **Actinomma. Thalassicolla,** no skeleton. **Collozoum,** colonial and without skeleton. **Acanthometra. Eucyrtidium.**

Class II. Infusoria (Plegepoda).

Protozoans with a definitely-shaped body invested by a cuticle Locomotion effected, and food- and oxygen-bearing currents produced by vibratile membranes, flagella, or cilia.

Order 1. *Flagellata* (Mastigophora). With one or more flagella, and a contractile vacuole. Reception of food effected by short broad pseudopodia, or through a cell-mouth. Some possess chlorophyll, and then live partly or entirely (holophytic) like green plants. Reproduction by longitudinal fission or by spores. Conjugation frequent. **Monas, Cercomonas, Uroglena. Bodo. Euglena. Pandorina, Volvox, Haematococcus,** holophytic, and first two colonial. **Codosiga,** with single flagellum surrounded by oral collar. **Ceratium, Peridinium,** and **Noctiluca,** marine forms, with shell and two flagella.

The lower Flagellates are allied by spore-formation and presence of flagella to the *Schizomycetes* (**Bacterium ; Leptothrix ; Cladothrix**), the higher to the *Ciliata*.

Order 2. *Ciliata* (= Infusoria in limited sense). Protozoans of stable form, with firm ectosarc (cortical layer), giving origin to variously disposed cilia which pierce the cuticle when present. Usually possess nucleus, paranucleus ; contractile vacuole ; mouth, gullet, and anal spot ; contractile fibres ; and sometimes bristles and stalks. Reproduction effected by fission, gemmation, and spore-formation. Permanent or temporary conjugation. Encystment.

Holotricha : body uniformly covered with short cilia, no adoral ciliated zone. **Paramœcium aurelia,** slipper animalcule ; **Opalina ranarum,** without mouth and anus, parasitic in rectum of frog.

Heterotricha : the entire body covered with cilia arranged in longitudinal rows, an adoral band of cilia present. **Stentor polymorphus** (cœruleus) ; **Balantidium** and **Nyctotherus** in rectum of frog.

Hypotricha : mouth and anus placed on the ventral surface which is provided with locomotor cilia and bristles, dorsal surface naked or with fine tactile cilia. **Stylonichia mytilus, Oxytricha gibba.**

Peritricha : cylindrical ; with an adoral spiral of cilia and frequently with a girdle of cilia. Longitudinal fission. **Vorticella nebulifera, V. microstoma, Carchesium, Epistylis,** bell animalcules, all stalked.

Order 3. *Suctoria* (Acinetaria, Tentaculifera). Usually fixed Infusorians, devoid of cilia in the adult condition, but possessing bundles of suctorial tentacles. Reproduction chiefly by internal gemmation, with production of free-swimming ciliated young. **Acineta, Podophrya gemmipara.**

Class III. Gregarinida (Sporozoa).

Mouthless unicellular endoparasites, with cortical layer and cuticle. Reproduction by spores (pseudonavicellæ) following conjugation and encystment. **Gregarina blattarum. Monocystis agilis** in vesiculæ seminales of Earthworm. **Psorosperms.**

Grade B. METAZOA (Enterozoa).

The unicellular Protozoa are contrasted with the remaining animals forming Grade B **METAZOA,** which possess cellular differentiated tissues and organs. Sexual reproduction by ova and spermatozoa. From the fertilized ovum a Blastula is produced by continued cell-division (cleavage), and from this a Gastrula with Ectoderm and Endoderm.

The probable phylogenetic connection of the Metazoan classes is shown in the following scheme; and several important typical differences are collected together in the annexed table:—

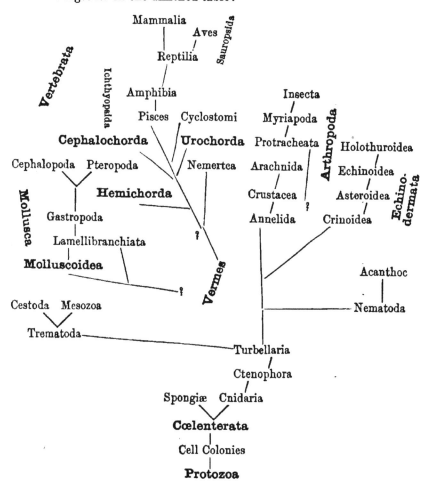

( ) = in a few or the minority of cases.	Body. r = radial. b = bilateral. s = segmented.		Gut. m = mouth. a = anus.	Nervous System. G = ganglion. R = ring round gullet. ∞ = many.	H = hermaphrodite. s = separate sexes.	P = parasites. f = free-living.
Spongiæ, . .	(r)		inhalent and exhalent apertures; canal system	scattered cells	H s	f
Cnidaria, . .	r	(b)	m; gastro-vascular sac	network, often plus ring or ∞ G	(H) s	f
Turbellaria, . .	b		m; tube, often branched	GG	H (s)	f
Nemertina, . .	b		m, a, tube	GG	(H) s	f
Trematoda, . .	b		m, forked tube	GG (R)	H	P
Cestoda, . .	b, often strobilized		nil	commissure in head, lateral cords	H	P
Nematoda, . .	b		m, a, tube	R	s	P f
Acanthocephala, .	b		nil	G	s	P
Rotatoria, . .	b		♀ m, a ♂ rudim.	G	s	
Annelida, . .	b	s	m, a	GG; ventral chain	(H) s	(P) f
Echinodermata, .	r larvae b		m, a or m only	R, radial nerves	(H) s	f
Arthropoda, . .	b	s	m, a	GG; ventral chain	(H) s	(P) f
Polyzoa, . .	b		m, a	G	H s	f
Brachiopoda, . .	b	s ?	m, a or m only	R, on which are variable number of G	(H) s	f
Mollusca, . .	b		m, a	R with three pairs of G	(H) s	(P) f
Balanoglossus, .	b		m, a	dorsal, partly hollow cord connected with ventral cord	s	f
Urochorda, . .	b	s	m, a	dorsal neural tube in Appendicularia and embryos, G. in most adults	H (s)	f
Cephalochorda, .	b	s	m, a	dorsal neural tube	s	f
Vertebrata, . .	b	s	m, a	dorsal neural tube	(H) s	(P) f

Reproduction may exhibit—					Blood Vascular System.		Special Respiratory Organs present.	m = marine. f = freshwater. l = land	
f = fission.	b = budding.	p = parthenogenesis.	m = metamorphosis.	a = alternation of generation.	o = open.	c = closed.			
f	b				·			almost all m	
(f)	b		m	a				almost all m	
(f)			(m)					m f l	
			(m)		(o)	c	Ciliated pits in head	almost all m	
	b		m	a					
f	b		m	a					
								(m) f	
		p					trochal apparatus ?	mostly f	
(f)			m		o in Hirudinea c in Chætopoda and Gephyrea		often gills	mostly m (f) (l)	
(f)			(m)			c	water-vascular system	m	
		(p)	(m)		o		gills, lung-books, tracheæ	m f l	
	b		m			c in Phoronis, absent elsewhere	lophophore	m (f)	
			m		o presence disputed		lophophore	m	
			(m)		o		gills, lungs	m f l	
			m			c	perforated pharynx	m	
	b		m	(a)	o		perforated pharynx	m	
						c	perforated pharynx	m	
			(m)			c	ditto, with gill-filaments; lungs, allantois.	m f l	

Subgrade A.   *CŒLENTERATA* (Diploblastica).

Metazoans of prevailing radial symmetry, with wide digestive cavity (gastrovascular system). No body-cavity (as blood or lymph-reservoir). Ectoderm and endoderm separated by a supporting lamella (mesoglœa). Asexual reproduction often obtains (gemmation, fission, frequently leading to formation of stocks). The development usually exhibits a metamorphosis (with planula larva), and often an alternation of generations (sexual and asexual generations alternating). With few exceptions (Spongilla, Hydra, &c.), marine.

B

Phylum I. SPONGIÆ (Porifera). Sponges.

The digestive tract has the form of a much-branched canal-system. Many of the endoderm cells (collar-cells), which may be limited to flagellated chambers, are provided with a flagellum and collar. Numerous microscopic pores (inhalent or nutritive apertures), and one or more oscula (exhalent apertures). The mesogloea contains sense-cells, contractile fibrous cells, supporting cells, skeletogenous cells (together with horny fibres, and calcareous or siliceous spicules), pigment cells, wandering cells, ova, and spermatozoa. Asexual reproduction by budding, through gemmules, &c. Sexes mostly separated; usually viviparous. Thread-cells absent, in contrast to the Cnidaria. Marine, with few exceptions.

Order 1. *Silicospongiæ* (Fibrospongiæ, Micromastictora). Usually possess a skeleton of horny fibres, siliceous spicules, or both. Collar-cells small.

Tetractinellidæ (Lithospongiæ), siliceous sponges with 4-rayed spicules. **Geodia, Monactinellidæ.**

Hexactinellidæ (Hyalospongiæ), 6-rayed siliceous spicules. **Euplectella,** Venus' flower-basket; **Hyalonema,** glass-rope sponge.

Halichondriæ, skeleton of horny fibres and siliceous spicules. **Reniera, Spongilla fluviatilis,** fresh-water sponge.

Ceratospongiæ, horny sponges. **Euspongia officinalis adriatica,** bath sponge.

Myxospongiæ, gelatinous sponges, without skeleton. **Halisarca lobularis.**

Order 2. *Calcispongiæ,* calcareous sponges. **Grantia, Leuconia, Sycon.**

Phylum II.　CNIDARIA (Nematophora).

Radial animals without pore-canals, and with thread-cells (or adhesive cells) in their epithelium.　Nerves and sense-organs.

Class I.　Hydrozoa (Polypomedusæ).

Polypes and medusæ with digestive cavity sac-like, or narrowed (gastro-vascular space).　No gullet (stomodæum).　Development chiefly by alternation of generations (medusoid sexual generation, or free-swimming medusæ as sexual animals).

Order 1. *Hydromedusæ.*　Hydroid stocks devoid of mesenteric folds, and with sexual medusoid buds or small craspedote medusæ as sexual animals.　The nursing hydroid stock often possesses a horny cuticular skeleton (perisarc); the sexual hydromedusæ mostly small, with only 4, 6, or 8 radial vessels, muscular velum, naked marginal sense organs, —eye-spots (Ocellatæ), or otocysts (Vesiculatæ), double marginal nerve-ring, and sexes usually separate.　The blastula formed by delamination.

Gymnoblastea - Anthomedusæ, perisarc stops short at bases of polypes; medusæ with ocelli, and with genital organs in the manubrium.　**Hydra viridis, H. fusca,** solitary freshwater hermaphrodites, devoid of perisarc or medusoid buds.　**Cordylophora lacustris,** the sexual buds remain attached.　**Eudendrium. Syncoryne sarsii,** with **Sarsia tubulosa** as medusa.　**Hydractinia** and **Tubularia,** medusæ attached.　**Cœnograptus,** Ordovician.　**Ctenaria ctenophora,** a transitional form to the Ctenophora.

Calyptoblastea - Leptomedusæ, perisarc forms hydrothecæ and gonangia; medusæ with ocelli or otocysts, and genital organs in the course of the radial canals.　**Sertularia** and **Plumularia** with attached, **Campanularia** and **Obelia** with free medusæ.　**Æquorea,** large medusa with numerous radial vessels and marginal tentacles.

Trachymedusæ, craspedote medusæ without gastral filaments, and with a velum.　Dense gelatinous umbrella.　Sense-organs as tentaculocysts.　The asexual hydroid generation has fallen out.　**Ægina** and **Geryonia** with 6, **Liriope** with 4 radial canals.　The freshwater medusa, **Limnocodium** (? with a hydroid stage), possibly belongs here.

Hydrocorallinæ, polymorphic colonies with calcified cuticular skeleton; medusoid stage represented by sporosacs.　**Millepora. Stylaster.**

Order 2. *Siphonophora,* free-swimming polymorphic stocks.　**Physophora hydrostatica. Physalia pelagica,** Portuguese man-of-war. **Diphyes. Velella.**

Order 3. *Acalephæ* (Scyphomedusæ, Acraspeda).　Medusæ with gastral filaments, lappets to umbrella, covered marginal sense-organs (tentaculocysts), and central nervous system in the form of groups of ganglion-cells. No velum. Development seldom direct (Pelagia, Charybdeidæ ?), usually with alternation of generations, the asexual generation being a short broad scyphistoma, which strobilizes to produce medusæ. The blastula formed by invagination.

C a l y c o z o a (Lucernariæ), fixed scyphistoma form without medusoid stage. **Lucernaria.**

M a r s u p i a l i d a, a high arched umbrella with 4-divided margin, four interradial tentacles, a pseud-velum, and four gastric pouches with four lamellar genital glands on the partitions separating them. **Charybdæa.**

D i s c o m e d u s æ (Discophora), discoid acraspedote medusæ with 8-divided umbrella-edge, slightly curved umbrella, genital glands in floor of stomach, and at least eight tentaculocysts situated in notches. Oral tentacles usually large. **Pelagia noctiluca. Aurelia aurita,** small, with branched radial vessels united by a ring-canal. **Rhizostoma Cuvieri,** without marginal filaments, but with dorsal and ventral oral frills ; the central mouth-opening of the Ephyra (young form) converted later by coalescing folds into numerous suctorial pores.

Class II. **Anthozoa** (Actinozoa). Corals.

Polypes with gullet (stomodæum), which is fixed to the body-wall by mesenteries, which bear mesenteric filaments and the endodermal genital glands. Sexes generally separated. A crown of hollow tentacles surrounds the elongated mouth. Usually with a firm calcareous non-superficial skeleton, and frequently colonial by budding. For the most part inhabitants of shallow water (coral reefs).

Order 1. *Rugosa* (Tetracoralla). Palæozoic (except **Holocystis**) corals, with numerous tetramerously grouped septa. **Cyathophyllum.**

Order 2. *Alcyonaria* (Octactinia, Octocoralla), with eight pinnate tentacles, and as many uncalcified mesenteric folds with ventral retractor muscles. Calcareous spicules usually present in the mesogloea.—**Alcyonium digitatum,** dead man's fingers, stocks of fleshy polypes.—**Pennatula rubra** and **Veretillum,** sea-pens, stocks, of which the naked basis sticks in the mud, horny axial skeleton ; the latter diœcious. **Gorgonia ; Corallium rubrum,** red coral. **Tubipora purpurea,** organ-pipe coral. **Heliopora,** massive skeleton, dimorphic polypes.

Order 3. *Zoantharia* (Hexactinia, Hexacoralla). The number of the non-pinnate tentacles, and mesenteric pouches, six, or a multiple thereof. Mesenteries usually paired, and the retractor muscles not arranged as in Alcyonaria. Generally a compact skeleton.—**Actinia mesembryanthemum,** sea anemone, a solitary form with several alternating circlets of tentacles ; fixed by an adhesive disc ; **Cerianthus,** elongated with an aboral pore ; hermaphrodite.—**Antipathes,** with six tentacles and a horny skeletal axis.

We group together as M a d r e p o r a r i a the forms with a firm calcareous skeleton. Aporosa : **Caryophyllæa. Oculina virginea. Astræa. Mæandrina,** brain coral. **Fungia discus,** mushroom coral. Perforata : **Madrepora cervicornis. Asteroides.**

Class III. **Ctenophora.**

Free-swimming hermaphrodites with eight rows of external ciliary plates, with gullet (stomodæum) and gastro-vascular canals arranged bilaterally. Usually with two retractile tentacles. Thread-cells replaced by adhesive cells. **Cydippe. Cestus Veneris. Beroe Forskâlii. Cœloplana,** a creeping form.

Subgrade B. *CŒLOMATA*. (Triploblastica).

Bilaterally symmetrical forms with a præoral region (head). A third cellular body-layer, the mesoderm, present between the embryonic ectoderm and mesoderm. Within this a body-cavity (cœlom) is usually developed outside the digestive cavity.

.

Phylum I. VERMES. Worms.

Bilateral forms with unsegmented or segmented body, paired excretory organs, dermal musculature, &c. A sharp diagnosis of this group is the less easy, since it not only contains the most different forms, but also connecting links with all the higher phyla. The lower worms (Turbellaria) similarly connect themselves with the Cœlenterata (Ctenophora).

The group of Vermes has long been made a receptacle for all sorts of doubtful forms, and, since the removal of the Tunicata from the Molluscoidea, the Polyzoa and Brachiopoda have usually been added to it. Ray Lankester abandons both Vermes and Molluscoidea, and places their classes in separate phyla.

(1.) Platyhelmia. (Leeches are included here as well as ordinary flatworms.)

(2.) Nematoidea (including Nematoda and Chætognatha).

(3.) Acanthocephala.

(4.) Gastrotricha.

(5.) Podaxonia (Gephyrea + Polyzoa + Brachiopoda).

(6.) Appendiculata, see p. 62.—Tr.

Class I. **Platyhelmia** (Platyhelminthes). Flat-Worms.

Unsegmented worms, generally with flattened bodies. Body-cavity imperfectly developed (mesoderm generally parenchymatous), and usually an excretory system of longitudinal trunks with narrow branches. Cerebral ganglia generally present, but never a ventral nerve-cord. Mostly hermaphrodite. Many forms parasitic.

Order 1. *Turbellaria.* Free-living flat-worms, with soft, ciliated, trichocyst-bearing skin. Mouth and muscular pharynx, but no anus. Live in water or damp places.

R h a b d o c œ l i d a, small forms with intestine, when present, a simple tube. **Convoluta,** no intestine. **Micr stomum,** fission, stiff tactile hairs ; **Vortex, Monotus.**

D e n d r o c œ l i d a, large forms, with branched intestine and follicular testes. (*a*) Triclades (Monogonopora), elongated Dendrocœles with three main divisions to intestine, and single genital opening. Land (**Geodesmus** in pot-earth ; **Bipalium**) and freshwater (**Planaria torva, P. dioica ; Dendrocœlum lacteum**) Planarians. **Gunda** (internal organs segmentally arranged), marine. (*b*) Polyclades (Digonopora), flattened leaf-like marine Dendrocœles, with a central stomach and two genital openings. **Leptoplana tremellaris ; Thysanozoon** (metamorphosis with Müller's larva) ; both marine.

Order 2. *Nemertina* (Nemertea). Elongated ciliated worms with a dorsal eversible proboscis (surrounded by nervous commissures), a straight gut terminating in an anus, blood-vessels and spaces (body-cavity), a pair of cephalic pits and two anterior nephridia. Nearly all marine, and with sexes separate.

A n o p l a, proboscis devoid of armature, three layers of muscle in body-wall, and development sometimes with metamorphosis (larva of Desor, and Pilidium). **Lineus longissimus. Borlasia. Pelagonemertes.**

E n o p l a (Hoplonemertea), proboscis armed with stylets, two layers of muscle in body-wall, development direct. **Nemertes. Tetrastemma obscura,** viviparous. **Malacobdella.**

Order 3. *Trematoda.* Flukes. Parasites with mouth-opening placed in an anterior sucker, forked or branched aproctous intestine, and supra-pharyngeal ganglia. Usually provided with organs of adhesion in addition to the anterior sucker. Nearly all hermaphrodite [typical parts, —two testes with vasa deferentia, cirrus-sac with cirrus. Ovary (germarium), two yolk-glands (vitellaria), oviduct, ootype with copulatory passage (Laurer's canal), shell-glands]. Mostly oviparous.

D i s t o m e æ—endoparasites with not more than two suckers. Development with metamorphosis and alternation of generations. [From the egg an embryo, usually ciliated, is developed, generally in water. This penetrates into an intermediate host (usually a mollusc), and develops into a redia (with mouth and gut) or sporocyst (without gut), which indirectly or directly produces cercariæ (tailed, with forked intestine). The cercaria, often after a second migration into another invertebrate host (*e.g.*, a water-snail), ultimately reaches the final host (a vertebrate) in which the sexual form is attained]. **Distomum hepaticum** (Fasciola hepatica), liver-fluke. Body covered with chitinous prickles. In the bile-ducts of the sheep and other domestic animals, occasionally of man. Ciliated aquatic embryo, with x-shaped eye spot; the asexual nurse-forms (sporocyst and redia) in Limnæus truncatulus. From the redia tailed cercariæ are developed, which become free and encyst on grass, &c., with which they are swallowed by the vertebrate host. **D. crassum**, in the intestine of the Chinese. **D. hæmatobium** (Bilharzia), bisexual; in the portal, mesenteric, and vesical veins of the Abyssinians. **Monostomum flavum**, in water birds, the young form (Cercaria ephemera) in Planorbis.

P o l y s t o m e æ,—mostly ectoparasites with more than two suckers. Development direct, or without considerable metamorphosis. **Polystomum integerrimum**, in the urinary bladder of the frog. Egg production commences in the spring (mutual fertilization), and the larva, which is hatched in the water, enters the gill-chamber of a tadpole, loses its five ciliated bands, and passing down the alimentary canal reaches the bladder in eight weeks. Here it becomes sexually mature in three or more years. (It rarely reaches the sexual stage in the gill-cavity, in which case it dies after producing an egg.) **Diplozoön paradoxum**, on the gills of many freshwater fish; two separate animals (Diporpa) partially fuse to a compound individual; eggs with attachment threads; larva ciliated. **Gyrodactylus.**

D

Order 4. *Cestoda.* Tape-worms. Elongated endoparasites, without gut or sense-organs, but with an attachment apparatus at the anterior end. Excretory organs consist of longitudinal canals, with branched canalettes. Hermaphrodite (numerous testes, with vas deferens, cirrus, and cirrus-sac. Ovaries, yolk-glands, spermatheca, shell-glands, uterus, and vagina). Numerous sets of reproductive organs usually present, contained in generative "segments" (proglottides) budded off from an anterior head. With advancing ripeness the male organs disappear; then the female organs with the exception of the exit passages. Two nerve-trunks, united in the head. Development seldom direct or with alternation of generations, mostly with a metamorphosis. The eggs generally reach dung-heaps or water, then enter with the food the stomach of omnivorous or plant-eating animals, where the egg-shells are ruptured; the freed six- (rarely four-) hooked embryos bore into the blood-vessels, and develop in the liver, lungs, brain, or muscles to encysted *measles* (bladder-worm, cysticercus, cysticercoid, cœnurus, echinococcus); after passive removal into the intestine of a carnivorous, insectivorous, or omnivorous animal, the everted bladder-worm (scolex) fixes itself firmly to the intestinal wall and grows into a jointed form (strobila).— **Caryophyllæus mutabilis,** non-jointed, in the intestine of Cyprinoids; young form in Tubifex rivulorum. **Archigetes Sieboldii,** non-jointed, with direct development, in body-cavity of Tubifex rivulorum.—**Bothriocephalus** with two adhesive pits, young form a scolex; genital openings in the middle of the ventral surface of the proglottis. **B. latus,** 24 to 30 feet long; in Russia, Poland, Switzerland, and S. France. The eggs, enclosed in shells, hatch in water, the ciliated embryo enters a first intermediate host, and with this as a scolex into the intestine of the pike or burbot. **B. cordatus,** 3 feet long, in the intestines of dog and man in Greenland. **Triænophorus nodulosus** in the intestine of the pike, young form in liver of carp.—**Ligula simplicissima,** non-jointed, in the intestine of water-fowls, and the body-cavity of fishes.—**Tænia solium,** two to three metres long, with four suckers and a double circlet of (26) hooks; in the intestine of man. Young form (measles, Cysticercus cellulosæ) in the muscles and subcutaneous connective tissue of swine, seldom of deer, dog, and cat, occasionally in muscles, eye, or brain of man (self-infection). **T. saginata** (mediocanellata), in the intestine of man, without circlet of hooks; four metres long; measles in muscles of the ox. **T. cœnurus,** in intestine of sheep-dog; young form in brain of one year old sheep (seldom in the body-cavity of rabbit, &c.) as Cœnurus cerebralis, the stagger-worm; (from the walls of the measles *numerous* tape-worm heads bud out. Alternation of generations). **T. echinococcus,** in the intestine of the dog, three to four millimetres long, forming but few proglottides. The corresponding bladder-worm with budding secondary and tertiary cysts in the liver and lungs of domestic animals (Echinococcus veterinorum, E. scolicipariens), or of man (E. hominis, E. altricipariens).

Order 5. *Mesozoa.* Multicellular endoparasites of small size and extremely simple structure. A ciliated ectoderm, and an endoderm of one or several cells giving rise to the genital products. Sexes separate. No mesoderm. Probably degenerate. Systematic position doubtful.

D i c y e m i d æ (Rhombozoa). A single endoderm cell. The male (infusoriform embryo) top-shaped. The females either *monogenic* or *diphygenic, i.e.,* producing females only, or females at first and then males. **Dicyema** (in cuttle-fishes, Octopus, Sepia).

O r t h o n e c t i d æ. Endoderm of several cells, some originating muscle-fibres, and others sexual products. The male elongated and annulated. The female dimorphic (annulated cylindrical female, flat female) and oviparous. **Rhopalura Giardi**, in the genital pouches of the Ophiuroid Amphiura squamata.

Class II. Nemathelmia (Nemathelminthes). Round-Worms.

Body cylindrical, unsegmented, devoid of lateral locomotor appendages, with papillæ or armature of hooks at the anterior end. No blood-vessels nor specialized respiratory organs. Predominantly parasitic. Sexes separate. Development generally without metamorphosis.

Order 1. *Nematoda.* Thread-worms. Usually possess a straight alimentary canal, and paired excretory tubes contained in lateral lines and opening by a ventral pore behind the terminal mouth. The male with curved tail-end and copulatory spicules, smaller than the female. The young form often inhabits an intermediate host.—**Ascaris lumbricoides,** round-worm of man (and as a smaller variety in swine); the transference probably takes place by an intermediate host (Julus guttulatus ?). **A. mystax,** in the cat and dog, occasionally in man. **A. megalocephala,** in the horse and ox. **Oxyuris vermicularis,** thread-worm, in the large intestine of man ; the female ten millimetres long.—**Strongylus. Rhabdonema nigrovenosa,** as a viviparous hermaphrodite in the frog's lung, producing a generation with separate sexes (Rhabditis), which becomes sexually mature in damp earth (heteromorphous generation). **Dochmius duodenalis,** 16 millimetres long ; in the small intestine of man, in Europe, Egypt, Comoro Islands, Brazil, and Cayenne. —**Trichocephalus dispar,** whip-worm, in the human colon ; transfer without intermediate host by filthy food. **Trichina spiralis,** in the intestine of man and other omnivorous mammals. The viviparous female trichina of the intestine, about eight days after its introduction, begins to bear young, which penetrate the wall of the intestine and make their way actively or by means of the blood-stream, into the muscles, here within fourteen days to develop into spiral worms and to encyst ; they first attain sexual maturity in the intestine of some other warm-blooded animal. This form is maintained by means of the house-rat.—**Filaria** (Dracunculus) **medinensis,** Guinea-worm, in the subcutaneous connective tissue of man ; the young form in Cyclops.—**Mermis,** devoid of anus, in the body-cavity of insects, thence to damp earth, where sexual maturity is reached.—**Sphærularia bombi,** in female humble-bees which survive the winter.—**Gordius aquaticus,** in insect larvæ, later in the body-cavity of predatory insects ; then becomes mouthless and sexually mature in water.—**Anguillula aceti,** vinegar-eel, free-living. **Tylenchus tritici,** in wheat, &c., causing ear-cockle; young form in earth.—**Dorylaimus,** common in mud.

Order 2. *Acanthocephala.* Endoparasites without mouth or alimentary canal. Possess a retractile hook-bearing proboscis. Sexes separate. A single genus **Echinorhynchus**. **E. gigas** in the small intestine of the pig ; the embryo is developed in the larva of the cockchafer.

The systematic position is doubtful of

Order 3. *Chætognatha*. Marine, free-living hermaphrodites with lateral fins, head, cerebral, sub-œsophageal and ventral ganglia. Are entero-cœlic (mesoderm developed from archenteric diverticula). **Sagitta germanica. S. bipunctata.**

Name.	Dwelling-place of Sexual Form.
Distomum hepaticum.	♂ ♀ in bile-ducts of sheep, other domestic mammals, seldom Man.
D. crassum.	♂ ♀ ditto, very rarely Man.
D. lanceolatum.	♂ ♀ ditto.
D. hæmatobium (Bilharzia).	♂ ♀ in portal vein, &c., of Man (Abyssinia); seldom in apes.
Monostomum flavum.	♂ ♀ in water-birds.
Polystomum integerrimum.	♂ ♀ urinary bladder of frog.
Diplozoon paradoxum.	♂ ♀ gills of freshwater fish.
Bothriocephalus latus.	♂ ♀ intestine of Man; rarely cat and dog.
Bothr. cordatus.	♂ ♀ intestine of dog and seal, seldom of Man.
Triænophorus nodulosus.	♂ ♀ intestine of pike.
Tænia solium.	♂ ♀ in the small intestine of Man.
T. saginata (mediocanellata).	♂ ♀ in the small intestine of Man.
T. cœnurus.	♂ ♀ in the intestine of sheep-dog.
T. echinococcus.	♂ ♀ in the small intestine of the dog.
Ascaris lumbricoides.	♂ ♀ in the small intestine of Man, ox, pig.
Asc. mystax.	♂ ♀ in intestine of cat and dog; very rarely Man.
Oxyuris vermicularis.	♂ ♀ in large intestine of Man.
Dochmius duodenalis.	♂ ♀ in small intestine of Man, gorilla.
Trichocephalus dispar.	♂ ♀ cæcum of Man, also in swine.
Trichina spiralis.	♂ ♀ small intestine of Man, rat, mouse, pig, cat, &c.
Filaria (Dracunculus) medinensis.	♂ ♀ in subcutaneous connective tissue of Man.
Gordius aquaticus.	♂ ♀ in water.
Rhabdonema nigrovenosa.	♂ ♀ lung parasites of Batrachians.
Echinorhynchus gigas.	♂ ♀ intestine of swine, Man.
Ech. proteus.	♂ ♀ intestine of freshwater fish.

Young Stages. I = Intermediate Host.	Distribution.
I; embryo (aquatic) bores into Limnæus truncatulus; sporocyst → redia → cercaria, the last encysts on grass, &c.	Europe, N. Africa, N. America, Australia.
I; ?	East Asia.
I; embryo (aquatic) penetrates Planorbis marginatus; sporocyst → redia → cercaria, the last encysts in Planorbis (?)	Europe and N. America.
I; embryo ciliated; further history unknown.	Cairo. The Cape.
I; as Cercaria ephemera in Planorbis.	
No I; larva on tadpole, resembles Gyrodactylus.	
No I; larva solitary (Diporpa).	
I; the ciliated embryo appears to pass into a first I, from thence (by intestine, &c.) into muscles of pike and burbot.	West Switzerland and S. France, Russian Baltic Provinces, Sweden, &c.; rarely Germany, Japan.
I; undoubtedly fish.	Greenland, Iceland.
I; encysted in the liver of Cyprinus.	
I; the pig, rarely Man (self-infection), dog, cat. Cysticercus cellulosæ.	
I; the ox.	
I; as Cœnurus cerebralis in the brain of sheep.	
I; domestic animals, more rarely Man.	Iceland, Europe, India, &c.
I probably; (Julus guttulatus?); the eggs pass into water.	Cosmopolite.
Apparently no I.	
No I; self-infection.	
No I; young form (Rhabditis) lives free in mud.	Switzerland, Italy, Egypt, Comoro Islands, Brazil, Cayenne.
Apparently no I; young free-living?	Widely distributed.
No I; the young forms encyst in the infected animals.	
I; the young form in Cyclops.	Tropics of the Old World, West Indies.
I; embryos pass into insects, later into predatory insects, become sexual in water.	
♂ ♀ in damp earth (Rhabditis).	
I; pass into cockchafer larvæ.	
I; encyst in Gammarus pulex.	

Class III. **Rotatoria** (Rotifera). Wheel Animalcules.

Small unsegmented aquatic animals. Possess a retractile trochal apparatus, a single cerebral ganglion, and two excretory tubes opening into an archicœlic body-cavity; sexes separate. No vascular system. The male smaller, mostly with a cord-like rudiment of the gut, and mouthless. Summer eggs (parthenogenetic), and winter eggs (fertilized).—**Rotifer vulgaris** (redivivus), trochal disc double. **Brachionus** with carapace. **Hydatina senta**. **Pedalion**, with limb-like appendages.

Here may be annexed the *Gastrotricha*, with ciliated ventral surface. **Chætonotus**.

Ray Lankester includes Rotatoria (on the strength of Pedalion), Chætopoda, and Arthropoda, in a single phylum,—Appendiculata, characterized by the possession of lateral locomotor appendages.—Tr.

Class IV. **Annelida** (Annulata). Ringed Worms.

Homonomously segmented worms, with brain, ventral chain of ganglia, closed vascular system, and paired nephridia (segmental organs). Typical larval form the trochosphere.

Order 1. *Archiannelida*, small marine worms, devoid of setæ and parapodia. Body-wall without a circular layer of muscle. **Polygordius** (with Lovén's larva). **Protodrilus. Histriodrilus** (Histriobdella). **Dinophilus.**

Order 2. *Chætopoda*, bristle-worms. Free-living forms, with a more or less prominent præstomium, and paired groups of setæ. Body-cavity entirely enterocœlic ; vascular system of a series of closed tubes.

P o l y c h æ t a, marine, with numerous setæ imbedded in parapodia. Antennæ, palpi, cirri, and gills generally present. Sexes usually separate, and development with a metamorphosis. **Nereis. Syllis. Aphrodite,** sea mouse. **Polynoe. Arenicola piscatorum,** lug-worm, **Terebella,** and **Serpula,** with tubes. **Myzostoma,** a small much-modified ecto-parasite, occurring on Crinoids.

O l i g o c h æ t a, fresh-water or terrestrial, with relatively few setæ. Devoid of antennæ, palpi, cirri, and gills. Hermaphrodites with direct development. **Lumbricus terrestris** (agricola), earthworm. **Lumbriculus variegatus. Nais proboscidea. Tubifex rivulorum.**

Order 3. *Hirudinea* (Discophora), leeches. Aquatic hermaphrodite ectoparasites divided into annuli more numerous than the true segments, some of which are fused posteriorly into a terminal sucker, dorsal to which is the anus. Mouth anterior, ventral, and surrounded by a sucker. Setæ and parapodia absent. Body-cavity in the form of vascular spaces in the connective tissue which occupies the space between body-wall and gut. **Piscicola geometra** (on freshwater fish) and **Clepsine** with protrusible proboscis. **Hirudo medicinalis** (var. officinalis), medicinal leech, with three toothed jaws ; attains sexual maturity in about three years.

E

Class V. **Gephyrea.**

Unsegmented marine worms, more or less cylindrical in form. There is a proboscis or the anterior end of the body is invaginable. Nervous system of a circumœsophageal loop (sometimes with a brain) and a ventral non-ganglionated cord. A large enterocœlic body-cavity, usually communicating with the exterior by a small number of anterior nephridia. Sexes separate.

A r m a t a (Chætifera), with a proboscis and two ventral setæ. Anus terminal. **Echiurus. Thalassema. Bonellia viridis** (dwarf planarian-like male, parasitic in the female).

I n e r m a (Achæta), with invaginable anterior end, and no setæ. **Sipunculus nudus. Phascolosoma vulgare. Priapulus.** The two first with dorsal anterior anus.

See note on p. 39.

Phylum II. ECHINODERMATA.

Radial marine animals with pentamerous symmetry (the larvæ bilaterally symmetrical), and with calcifications in the skin.   A water-vascular system typically composed of a ring-canal with connected stone-canal, Polian vesicles, tentacular tubes, and five ambulacral canals.   A nerve-ring with five main trunks, radial in position.   After complete (often regular) cleavage of the fertilized ovum a blastula with segmentation-cavity is formed, and from this a gastrula with the two germinal layers, ectoderm (epiblast) and endoderm (hypoblast).   The mesoderm and water-vascular system are formed from diverticula of the archenteron. The blood-vascular system is developed from spaces in the mesodermic tissue.   Body-cavity an enterocœle.   A metamorphosis.

Class I. **Crinoidea.** Sea Lilies.

Spherical, goblet- or cup-shaped; fixed when young or permanently by a jointed calcareous stalk. Possess branched arms, usually furnished with pinnules. A nervous system on the aboral side of the body, in addition to the ordinary one. Groups of tentacles are formed by side branches of the radial water-vascular vessels. No madreporic plate or stone-canal, but water-tubes opening into the enterocœlic body-cavity, which again communicate by water-pores with the exterior. Many fossil forms; recent examples mostly inhabitants of the deep sea. **Encrinus liliiformis** from the Muschelkalk. **Pentacrinus caput Medusæ**, recent. **Comatula** (Antedon) **rosacea**, feather star, stalked when young, later on free.

Class II. Asteroidea. Star-fish.

Body star-shaped or pentagonal; the tube-feet on the ventral surface.

Order 1. *Stellerida.* Digestive cæca, extending into the arms; anus dorsal when present. Tube-feet situated in ambulacral grooves, usually end in suckers; madreporic plate dorsal and interradial. Some develop directly in a brood-cavity of the mother, the rest with a metamorphosis (Bipinnaria, Brachiolaria). Pedicellariæ. **Asterias** (Uraster) **rubens,** common star-fish, and **A. glacialis,** tube-feet in four rows. **Solaster papposus,** sun-star, generally with thirteen arms. **Astropecten auran-tiacus,** tube-feet without suckers, in two rows. **Asterina gibbosa,** pentagonal.

Order 2. *Ophiurida,* brittle stars. Arms cylindrical, sharply marked off from body; stomach without cæcal prolongations. Ambulacral furrows covered in by dermal plates, so that the tube-feet, which are devoid of suckers, protrude at the sides of the arms. No anus; no pedicellariæ (as a rule). Madreporic plate ventral, usually fused to an oral plate. Larval form a Pluteus. **Ophiothrix fragilis** and **Amphiura squamata,** viviparous. **Astrophyton arborescens** with soft-skinned ventral surface, branched arms, and pedicellariæ.

Class III. Echinoidea. Sea-urchins.

Body rounded or flattened. Twenty rows of calcareous dermal plates make up a strong test, perforated by rows of tube-feet, and bearing movable spines and pedicellariæ. Tube-feet with suckers. Blood-vascular system often well developed. The genital pores lie at the vertex (periproct) of the shell on interradial genital plates one of which is the madreporic plate; radial ocular plates alternate with the preceding. The mouth of the gastrula persists as the anus. Development with a Pluteus larva. Many occur fossil.

Order 1. *Regularia.* Spherical, with masticatory apparatus (Aristotle's lantern) of five oral teeth, &c. **Echinus melo, Toxopneustes, Strongylocentrotus lividus,** all with oral gills; **Cidaris,** without oral gills. **Calveria** (Asthenosoma), a deep-sea form with flexible test.

Order 2. *Clypeastroidea,* shield-urchins. Irregular, with central mouth and masticatory apparatus; around the aboral pole a five-leaved ambulacral rosette; anus excentric. **Clypeaster; Mellita** with fenestrated shell.

Order 3. *Spatangoidea,* heart-urchins. Irregular with excentric mouth and anus; no masticatory apparatus. **Spatangus purpureus** with four genital glands and openings.

Class IV. Holothuroidea. Sea-cucumbers.

Elongated forms with tough muscular body-wall containing calcareous bodies, and with a circlet of retractile oral tentacles. Gullet surrounded by a ring of calcareous ossicles. The madreporic plate external in the larvæ and also in many adult Elasipoda, but directed into the body-cavity in other adults. A blood-vascular system. Larva (Auricularia) most like that of Stellerida.

Order 1. *Pedata*, with respiratory trees, and external ambulacral appendages (tube-feet, papillæ), which are arranged in rows or scattered. Sexes separate.

D e n d r o c h i r o t æ, arborescent tentacles; five retractors to the pharynx ; generative cæca in two bundles. **Cucumaria Planci,** ten tentacles.

A s p i d o c h i r o t æ, 20–30 shield-shaped tentacles, by means of which the food is shovelled into the mouth ; only one bundle of generative cæca. **Holothuria tubulosa,** 20 tentacles ; **Mülleria,** 25 tentacles, five circumanal plates.

Order 2. *Elasipoda*, all primitive deep-sea forms, with reduced or rudimentary calcareous ring; without respiratory trees or ciliated funnels; stone-canal often opening to the exterior. Sexes separate. Move by creeping, and the dorsal and ventral surfaces sharply marked off in consequence ; tube-feet limited to the latter. **Deima,** the calcareous ring a brittle network, long stiff papillæ on the back.

Order 3. *Apoda*, without tube-feet or papillæ.
P n e u m o n o p h o r a, with respiratory trees. **Molpodia.**
A p n e u m o n a, ciliated funnels in the mesentery instead of respiratory trees; mostly hermaphrodite. **Chirodota,** with calcareous wheels in the skin. **Synapta digitata,** calcareous ossicles in the form of plates and anchors.

Phylum III. ARTHROPODA.

The heteronomously segmented body with jointed lateral appendages, brain and ventral ganglionated chain, and chitinous exoskeleton. Vascular system, when present, not closed, but communicates with the irregular spaces which make up the body-cavity.   Enterocœlic spaces inconspicuous.   Sexes almost always distinct.   Development frequently with metamorphosis ; sometimes parthenogenesis.

See note, p. 62.

Class I. Crustacea.

Aquatic forms usually breathing by gills, with two pairs of antennæ, with paired limbs on the thorax and usually on the abdomen.

On the head two pairs of antennæ, a labrum, two mandibles with palps, and two pairs of maxillæ. The thorax bears (at least three) pairs of appendages, of which some of the most anterior are frequently modified into foot-jaws (maxillipedes), while the following vary in form and function, as do the abdominal appendages. The typical larval form of the lower Crustaceans is the Nauplius, of the higher the Zoëa.

GROUP A. ENTOMOSTRACA. Small forms of simple structure, with a variable number of segments and appendages. Generally a Nauplius larva.

Order 1. *Phyllopoda.* With four or more pairs of leaf-shaped lobed swimming feet, and generally a carapace or bivalve shell. Mostly in freshwater lakes.

B r a n c h i o p o d a, relatively large, with saccular gills attached to the numerous swimming feet. Elongated heart. Generally a nauplius larva.—**Branchipus stagnalis. Apus cancriformis**, male very rare.

C l a d o c e r a, water fleas, laterally compressed and imperfectly segmented, with large locomotor second antennæ, generally with a bivalve shell. Heart short. Summer and winter eggs ; parthenogenesis. Rarely a larva. **Daphnia pulex. Leptodora,** nauplius from winter eggs.

Order 2. *Ostracoda.* With unsegmented body, rudimentary abdomen, and seven pairs of appendages. Enclosed in a bivalve shell.—**Cypridina serrato-striata,** fossil, **C. mediterranea,** recent. **Cypris fusca.**

Order 3. *Copepoda.* Usually well segmented ; devoid of a shell. Four to five pairs of biramous swimming feet on the thorax, abdomen without appendages.—**Cyclops coronatus,** without heart. Common in fresh water. **Ergasilus, Chondracanthus, Caligus, Lernæa, Lernæocora, Achtheres,** and **Anchorella,** degenerate parasites with piercing or sucking mouth-parts and stunted abdomen.—**Argulus foliaceus** on the carp and stickleback ; the second maxillæ are modified into suckers.

Order 4. *Cirripedia.* Sessile hermaphrodites with a duplicature of the skin (and a shell).—**Lepas anatifera,** ship barnacle.—**Balanus tintinnabulum,** acorn barnacle, fossil and recent.

As R h i z o c e p h a l a or S u c t o r i a we group together the parasitic forms in which segmentation and gut are absent. **Peltogaster paguri, Sacculina carcini.**

GROUP B. LEPTOSTRACA. Small marine Crustaceans, with five cephalic, eight free thoracic, and eight abdominal segments; a forked telson. Anterior part of body enclosed in a bivalve shell. Eight pairs of foliaceous swimming-feet attached to the thorax. Eyes compound, on short stalks. No larval stage. Only known genus, **Nebalia**.

The Crustacean head is often regarded as composed of *six* segments; the telson is possibly a segment.—TR.

GROUP C. MALACOSTRACA.   Crustaceans with five cephalic, eight thoracic, and six abdominal segments; a telson.

Order 1. *Arthrostraca* (Edriophthalmata).   Seven (rarely six) free thoracic segments and sessile lateral eyes.   No cephalothoracic [shield or larval form.

A m p h i p o d a, body laterally compressed; gills on the thoracic limbs.—**Gammarus pulex. Talitrus locusta,** sand-hopper. **Phronima. Caprella linearis. Cyamus ceti.**

I s o p o d a, with vertically flattened body and gill-bearing abdominal appendages. **Asellus aquaticus, Oniscus murarius,** wood-louse, **Armadillo vulgaris; Tanais dubius,** with two kinds of male.

Order 2. *Thoracostraca.*   A cephalothoracic shield and compound eyes which are generally stalked.

C u m a c e a, 4–5 free thoracic segments, two pairs of foot-jaws, no abdominal appendages in the female, sessile eyes.   **Cuma.**

S t o m a t o p o d a, short cephalothoracic shield, five pairs of foot-jaws, gills abdominal.   **Squilla mantis,** locust-crab.

S c h i z o p o d a, a large cephalothoracic shield, and eight pairs of biramous thoracic appendages.   **Mysis,** opossum-shrimp, with otocysts in the tail-flaps.

D e c a p o d a, large cephalothoracic shield.   Thoracic appendages consist of three pairs of foot-jaws, and five pairs of uniramous feet: (*a*) Macrura with long abdomen; **Palæmon,** prawn,—**Crangon vulgaris,** shrimp,—**Astacus fluviatilis,** cray-fish,—**Homarus vulgaris,** lobster, —**Palinurus vulgaris,** rock-lobster,—**Nephrops Norvegicus,** Norway lobster,—**Pagurus Bernhardus,** hermit-crab: (*b*) Brachyura with short abdomen; **Cancer pagurus,** edible crab,—**Carcinus mœnas,** shore-crab.

Class II. Arachnida.

Wingless Arthropoda with a cephalothorax, and four to six pairs of legs.

GROUP A. ARACHNIDA BRANCHIATA (Gigantostraca, Pœcilopoda). Aquatic gill-bearing Arachnidans.

Order 1. *Xiphosura.* A shield-shaped cephalothorax, with a single pair of chelate appendages in front of the mouth, and five pairs of legs with masticatory bases behind the mouth. The abdomen bears six pairs of appendages, of which the first are united to form a genital operculum, while the remainder are lamellar with numerous gill-folds. A spine-like telson. Two large facetted frontal eyes, and two central dorsal eyes. Mostly fossil. **Limulus,** first occurs in the lithographic slates (Middle Oolite). **L. polyphemus,** recent.

Order 2. *Eurypterina.* Extinct forms with small cephalothoracic shield, one pair of præoral appendages, and four pairs of legs with masticatory bases around the mouth. Abdomen of twelve segments, devoid of abdominal appendages (?), and ending in a broad telson.—**Eurypterus pygmæus,** Devonian.

Order 3. *Trilobita.* Extinct forms with a cephalothoracic shield, no præoral appendages, but four pairs around the mouth. Abdomen bearing appendages, and with a segmented anterior region. **Calymene Blumenbachii. Phacops.**

GROUP B. ARACHNIDA TRACHEATA. Chiefly terrestrial Arachnidans, with cheliceræ (falces), pedipalpi, and 4 pairs of legs; but abdomen usually limbless. Breathe air by tracheæ, lung-books, or the skin.

Order 1. *Acarina*, mites. Abdomen fused with rest of body; respiration by skin or tracheæ.—**Demodex folliculorum,** hair-sheath mite, hermaphrodite. **Sarcoptes scabiei,** itch-mite, with suctorial cone and pincer-shaped cheliceræ. The females dig deep burrows in the epidermis, in which they live; hexapod larvæ. **Tyroglyphus siro,** cheese-mite. **Ixodes ricinus,** with tracheæ and two stigmata. **Hydrachna cruenta,** the six-legged larvæ parasitic on aquatic insects.

Order 2. *Pycnogonida* (Pantopoda). Marine forms of doubtful affinities, with rudimentary abdomen, and four pairs of walking legs. Cutaneous respiration. **Pycnogonum littorale.**

Order 3. *Tardigrada*, water-bears. Minute aquatic hermaphrodites, with piercing and sucking mouth parts, and four pairs of short walking legs. Devoid of circulatory and respiratory organs. **Macrobiotus Hufelandii.**

Order 4. *Linguatulidæ.* Parasites without tracheæ. Sexes separate. **Pentastomum tænioides** in the nasal cavities and frontal sinus of the wolf and dog. The embryos pass on to herbage and with this into the stomachs of the hare and rabbit, also of man, perforate the intestinal wall, encyst themselves in the liver, and lastly reach the final host with the flesh.

Order 5. *Araneida*, spiders. With poison-glands in the subchelate cheliceræ, pedipalps ambulatory, abdomen unsegmented. Two or four lung-books, six or four spinning papillæ.—Four lung-books: **Mygale avicularia. Cteniza cæmentaria** makes tubes with trap doors in the earth.—Two lung-books: **Salticus. Lycosa tarantula. Tegenaria domestica,** house spider. **Epeira diadema,** garden spider.

Order 6. *Phalangidæ*, harvestmen. With chelate cheliceræ, slender legs, and abdomen of six segments. Tracheate. **Phalangium opilio.**

Order 7. *Pedipalpi* (Phrynidæ). Clawed cheliceræ, large pedipalpi, slender first pair of legs, and two pairs of lung-books. Abdomen with eleven to twelve segments. **Phrynus.**

Order 8. *Scorpionidæ*, scorpions. With chelate cheliceræ, large chelate pedipalpi, four pairs of lung-books, and poison claw at the end of the tail. Abdomen with twelve segments and a telson; abdominal appendages as genital operculum and pectines. Lateral and central eyes. Viviparous.—**Scorpio Europæus. Androctonus.**

Order 9. *Pseudoscorpionidæ* (Chernelidæ). Small forms with large chelate pedipalpi and a broad flattened abdomen of 10–11 segments. Breathe by tracheæ. **Chelifer cancroides. Chernes.**

Order 10. *Solifugæ* (Solpugæ). Head distinct from the thorax, which has three segments; abdomen with nine segments. Chelate cheliceræ and leg-like pedipalpi. Breathe by tracheæ. **Galeodes** (Solpuga) **araneoides.**

Class III. **Protracheata** (Onychophora, Peripatidea).

Tracheates with vermiform body, two antennæ, a pair of jaws, a pair of oral papillæ, and numerous pairs of imperfectly jointed limbs. Stigmata numerous and scattered. Each foot-bearing segment with a pair of nephridia.—A single genus, **Peripatus**, which appears to be most closely allied to the Myriapods.

Class IV. **Myriapoda.**

Terrestrial Tracheates with numerous similar body-segments, a distinct head, a pair of antennæ, three pairs of jaws, and numerous paired legs.

Order 1. *Chilopoda*, centipedes. Body depressed, and only one pair of legs to each segment. A single posterior genital opening.—**Scolopendra morsitans. Geophilus electricus. Lithobius forficulatus.**

Order 2. *Chilognatha*, millipedes. Body rounded, and two pairs of legs to each segment. Genital openings on the basal joints of the second or third pair of limbs. **Julus sabulosus. Glomeris marginata.**

G

Class V. Insecta (Hexapoda).

Tracheates with distinct head, thorax and abdomen. The head bears a pair of antennæ, compound eyes, palpless mandibles, and two other pairs of jaws; the three thoracic segments bear three pairs of legs, and commonly one or two pairs of wings; abdomen usually limbless. At most ten pairs of stigmata. Sexes separate.

A. INCOMPLETE METAMORPHOSIS.

Order 1. *Orthoptera.* Jaws adapted for biting; two pairs of dissimilar wings. **Forficula,** earwig. **Periplaneta** (Blatta) **orientalis,** cockroach. **Phyllium, Phasma, Bacteria calamus,** and **Mantis religiosa** exhibit mimicry. **Œdipoda migratoria,** passage locust, **Locusta viridissima,** grasshopper. **Gryllotalpa vulgaris,** mole-cricket, **Gryllus campestris, G. domesticus,** house-cricket.

Order 2. *Thysanura* (Aptera), wingless. Body hairy or scaly. Mouthparts rudimentary. Tracheæ may be absent. **Podura. Lepisma saccharina. Campodea staphylinus** with foot-stumps on the anterior abdominal segments.

Order 3. *Pseudoneuroptera.* Mouth-parts biting; wings membranous, alike.—**Termes lucifugus,** white ant. **Thrips.**—Amphibiotic forms (the larvæ aquatic, with tracheal gills): **Ephemera vulgata,** May-fly. **Agrion puella, Æschna grandis, Libellula vulgata,** dragon flies.

Order 4. *Hemiptera.* Mouth-parts piercing or sucking.—**Coccus cacti,** cochineal insect, on Opuntia. **Aspidiotus nerii,** on Oleander. **Aphis rosae** with two honey-tubes; parthenogenesis in spring and summer. **Phylloxera vastatrix,** vine-louse, (from the winter-eggs wingless forms emerge in the spring, which destroy the vine-roots and reproduce parthenogenetically; later generations cause leaf-galls; the winged generation of late summer produce, parthenogenetically, dimorphic eggs from which large females and small asplanchnic males are hatched). **Cicada,** the abdomen of the male with a stridulating organ. **Acanthia** (Cimex) **lectularia,** bed-bug. **Nepa cinerea,** water-scorpion. **Pediculus capitis,** head-louse. **Phthirius vestimenti; P. pubis.**

B. COMPLETE METAMORPHOSIS.

Order 5. *Neuroptera.* Biting mouth-parts, free prothorax, and two pairs of similar membranous netted wings.—**Hemerobius perla,** lacefly. **Myrmeleon formicarius,** ant-lion.

Order 6. *Trichoptera* (Phryganidæ). Wings covered with hairs and scales; the larvæ aquatic, in tubular cases.—**Phryganea,** caddis-fly.

Order 7. *Strepsiptera.* Parasites, with rudimentary mouth-parts, the front wings of the male rudimentary and twisted, the female wingless and vermiform.—**Xenos vesparum. Stylops mellitæ.**

Order 8. *Diptera.* Mouth-parts sucking or piercing; front wings membranous, hind wings reduced to halteres.—Pupipara, the female produces larvæ ready to become pupæ. **Hippobosca equina.**—**Musca domestica,** house-fly. **M. vomitoria,** blue-bottle. **Sarcophaga carnaria,** flesh-fly, viviparous. **Gastrus equi,** bot-fly, larva in the wall of the horse's stomach. **Tabanus bovinus,** gad-fly.—Nemocera or Tipulariæ: **Corethra plumicornis,** larva with four tracheal bladders. **Culex pipiens,** gnat, the female stings. **Cecidomyia,** Hessian fly, and **Miastor,** viviparous. **Tipula,** crane-fly.

Order 9. *Aphaniptera,* fleas. Mouth-parts sucking and piercing. Wings rudimentary.—**Pulex irritans,** common flea.

Order 10. *Coleoptera,* beetles. With biting mouth-parts, horny front wings (elytra), and freely movable prothorax. Legs with five- rarely with four-jointed tarsi. **Coccinella septempunctata,** ladybird. **Cerambyx heros. Meloë proscarabæus,** oil beetle. **Lytta vesicatoria,** Spanish fly. **Lampyris noctiluca,** glow-worm. **Lucanus cervus,** stag beetle. **Melolontha vulgaris,** cockchafer. **Staphylinus. Hydrophilus piceus. Dytiscus marginalis.**

Order 11. *Hymenoptera.* Mouth-parts biting (or licking); four membranous wings.—Terebrantia, female with an ovipositor.—**Tenthredo,** saw-fly.—**Cynips quercus folii,** gall-fly. **Ichneumon.**—Aculeata, usually with a sting; young helpless.—**Formica rufa, fusca, rufescens, flava,** &c., ants. **Vespa vulgaris,** wasp. **Apus mellifica,** honey-bee, **Bombus terrestris,** humble-bee.

Order 12. *Lepidoptera,* moths and butterflies. With sucking mouth-parts, the maxillæ forming a rolled proboscis, and four scaly wings. Irregular parthenogenesis in several. **Tinea,** clothes-moth (one of the Microlepidoptera). **Geometra,** geometer. **Noctua. Bombyx mori,** silkworm moth, **Psyche helix,** both parthenogenetic. **Sphinx,** hawk-moth. **Sesia apiformis,** like a hornet (mimicry). **Picris brassicæ,** white cabbage butterfly. **Kallima paralecta** and **K. inachis,** both extremely like dry leaves when at rest.

Phylum IV. MOLLUSCOIDEA.

Sedentary, almost exclusively marine animals, with a lophophore bearing ciliated tentacles, an epistome, house or bivalve shell, and one or several ganglia. Præoral region much reduced or absent. Mouth and anus generally approximated. Body elongated at right angles to the oro-anal axis.

See note, p. 39.

Class I. Polyzoa (Bryozoa).

Small forms, usually colonial, and with sexes united. Development with a metamorphosis.

Order 1. *Vermiformia.* Social Polyzoans enclosed in leathery tubes ; lophophore horseshoe-shaped. Nervous system as a ring round the mouth and a body-nerve. A system of blood-vessels, enterocœlic body-cavity, and two nephridia. Only known genus **Phoronis**, with Actinotrocha larva.

Order 2. *Eupolyzoa.* Almost all colonial. Contained in cells formed by the thickened cuticle. Nervous system as a single ganglion. No vascular system. Budding always occurs.

E n d o p r o c t a. Anus within the lophophore, which can only be partially retracted. No proper body-cavity. Nephridia. **Pedicellina echinata**, colonial. **Loxosoma**, non-colonial.

E c t o p r o c t a : anus outside the lophophore, which can be completely retracted. An enterocœlic body-cavity.—**Cristatella, Plumatella, Alcyonella,** in fresh water, with horseshoe-shaped lophophore ; statoblasts. Tentacles in a circle in most marine forms : **Retepora, Membranipora, Flustra, Alcyonidium.**

Class II. Brachiopoda.

All marine, with bivalve shell (valves unequal, but symmetrical) and lophophore (horseshoe-shaped or in the form of two spiral arms). There is an enterocœlic body-cavity, and two or four nephridia. Larva vermiform. Mostly fossil.

Order 1. *Ecardines*, shell hingeless ; an anus. **Lingula antiqua. L. anatina,** recent.

Order 2. *Testicardines*, shell with hinge and (usually) a calcareous support for the arms ; no anus. **Productus,** fossil ; **Rhynchonella,** with short two-limbed, **Spirifera** (fossil) with spiral, **Terebratula** with loop-shaped arm-support. **Argiope.**

·

Phylum V. MOLLUSCA.

Unsegmented animals, with a soft body, mantle and dorsal shell (usually), muscular ventral foot, large digestive gland (liver), and open vascular system. Enterocœle represented by pericardial cavity, which typically communicates with exterior by a pair of nephridia. Cerebral, pleural, and pedal ganglia. Larva (Veliger) usually with a velum.

Subphylum *A.* Lipocephala (Acephala).

Head-region rudimentary and devoid of eyes. No odontophore.

Class I. Lamellibranchiata.

With bilobed mantle and shell (valves equal but unsymmetrical), large gill-plates (in most); two pairs of labial palps; paired nephridia (organs of Bojanus), auricles, digestive gland and gonads; sexes generally separate.

Order 1. *Asiphonida,* no siphons.—With one adductor muscle : **Pecten Jacobæus,** clam, **Ostrea edulis,** oyster, both hermaphrodite. With two adductors : **Meleagrina margaritifera,** pearl-mussel. **Mytilus edulis,** edible mussel. **Lithodomus dactylus. Trigonia. Unio pictorum, Anodonta cygnæa,** freshwater mussels (the free larva, "glochidium," parasitic on fishes).

Order 2. *Siphonida,* siphons; two adductor muscles. **Cardium edule,** cockle. **Cyclas cornea** in fresh water. **Venus. Solen Aspergillum,** with tubular shell. **Teredo navalis,** ship-worm.

Subphylum *B.*   Glossophora.

Head-region developed.   An odontophore.

Class I.   Scaphopoda.

Possess an ill-developed head, a trifid foot, and a curved tubular shell. Two bunches of gill-filaments, but no heart or eyes. Sexes separate and gonad unpaired. **Dentalium.**

Class II. Gastropoda.

The foot usually forms a simple sole-like ventral expansion.

A. *GASTROPODA ISOPLEURA.* Forms exhibiting bilateral sym-metry in the external form and in the arrangement of the auricles, ctenidia (gills), nephridia, genital ducts and nerve-cords. Anus posterior. Ganglia ill-developed.

Order 1. *Solenogastres* (Amphineura). Marine worm-like Molluscs with foot absent or rudimentary, and the body covered by calcareous spicules.—**Proneomenia. Neomenia. Chætoderma.**

Order 2. *Polyplacophora.* Eight calcareous plates along the back. **Chiton squamosus.**

B. *GASTROPODA ANISOPLEURA.* Head and foot bilaterally sym-metrical, but the visceral hump and mantle have undergone twisting so that the anus, nephridial opening, and genital opening are shifted more or less to the front. Generally a univalve shell, and a single auricle, ctenidium, nephridium, and genital duct.

Order 1. *Streptoneura* (Prosobranchia). Visceral nerve-loop twisted ; gills in front of the heart ; sexes separate. **Patella,** limpet (both ctenidia aborted, secondary gills), **Fissurella** and **Haliotis** with both ctenidia and two auricles; all three with paired nephridia. **Trochus** (rhipidoglossate). **Janthina** ptenoglossate). **Murex, Buccinum,** whelk, and **Purpura lapillus** (rhachiglossate). **Conus** (toxoglossate). The fol-lowing are tænioglossate : **Cyclostoma elegans** (lung-breathing), **Palu-dina vivipara,** river-snail, **Valvata** ($\frac{\delta}{+}$)—all fresh water : **Cypræa,** cowry, **Strombus ; Entoconcha mirabilis,** parasitic in Synapta ; **Am-pullaria,** with gill- and lung-chamber.

These forms are closely allied to the pelagic tænioglossate H e t e r o p o d a (Natantia) with fin-like foot: **Bellerophon,** fossil ; **Carinaria, Atlanta.**

Order 2. *Euthyneura.* Visceral nerve-loop not twisted. Hermaph-rodite.

(*a*) O p i s t h o b r a n c h i a, genital openings on the side of the body ; the branchial veins open behind the ventricle into the auricle ; larva with operculate shell, and velum. Shell usually absent in the adult: **Aplysia, Pleurobranchus, Bulla** (tectibranchs): **Phyllirhoë, Tethys, Doris, Æolis, Rhodope** (nudibranchs). **Elysia** (saccoglossate).

(*b*) P u l m o n a t a, hermaphrodites with a lung-chamber : Pul. basom-matophora, eyes at base of two non-invaginable tentacles : **Lymnæus stagnalis,** pond-snail, **L. truncatulus, Planorbis corneus,** trumpet-snail. Pul. stylommatophora, eyes at tips of two invaginable tentacles : **Arion ater,** black slug ; **Limax agrestis,** garden slug, **L. flavus,** cellar slug ; **Helix aspersa,** garden snail, **H. pomatia,** Roman snail, **H. nemoralis,** hedge snail.

Class III. Pteropoda.

(Form a transitional group to Cephalopoda.)

Marine hermaphrodite Molluscs, devoid of ctenidia, with the mid-foot produced into a pair of wing-like fins. Visceral hump large, and exhibiting secondary bilateral symmetry; anal, genital, and nephridial apertures anterior and lateral.

Order 1. *Thecosomata*, with shell; the fins not sharply marked off; a mantle-cavity, often containing branchial folds: **Hyalea tridentata, Cymbulia, Tentaculites** (fossil).

Order 2. *Gymnosomata*, without shell; fins sharply marked off; no mantle-cavity. Tentacles on the head. Larva with a zone of cilia: **Clio borealis. Pneumodermon**, two arms covered with suckers.

Class IV. Cephalopoda (Siphonopoda).

Marine; fore-foot united with head and forming tentacles or arms surrounding the mouth; mid-foot funnel-like; sexes separate. A large visceral hump and a mantle cavity containing two or four ctenidia and the anal, genital, and paired nephridial apertures. Chromatophores in the skin.

Order 1. *Tetrabranchiata*, two pairs of ctenidia and nephridia, numerous sheathed tentacles without suckers, and an external chambered shell. Funnel incompletely closed; no ink-bag.

Nautilidæ, septa of the shell concave, siphon central: **Orthoceras** and **Phragmoceras**, fossil; **Nautilus pompilius**, pearly nautilus, recent.

Ammonitidæ, septa much folded at their edges, siphon external; all fossil: **Goniatites, Ammonites** (with aptychus and anaptychus), **Ceratites nodosus, Baculites, Toxoceras, Hamites.**

Order 2. *Dibranchiata*, a single pair of ctenidia and nephridia, eight or ten arms covered with hooks or suckers, a completely closed funnel and an ink-bag.

Decapoda, ten arms, two of them much elongated; suckers stalked and with a horny ring. Body with two lateral fins, shell internal: **Belemnites** (fossil). **Spirula. Sepia officinalis,** cuttlefish. **Loligo vulgaris,** squid. **Sepiola vulgaris. Onychoteuthis.**

Octopoda, eight arms, suckers unstalked and without a horny ring, no internal shell, mantle cavity without a cartilaginous closing apparatus. **Octopus vulgaris, Eledone moschata. Argonauta argo,** paper nautilus; the female large, with a thin boat-shaped shell, secreted by the two dorsal arms; male small, without shell, and with one arm hectocotylized.

Phylum VI. CHORDATA.

Cœlomate animals with the neural and hæmal surfaces dorsal and ventral respectively. At some stage or other a cellular supporting rod, the notochord, underlies the central nervous system for part or all of its extent, and the pharynx is perforated by two or more gill-slits.

The term *Vertebrata* is often applied in a wide sense to this phylum. All other animals can then be lumped together under the name *Invertebrata*.

Subphylum A. Hemichorda.

Chordata with a short notochord mainly situated in the præstomium.—**Balanoglossus**, a worm-like marine form with præoral contractile proboscis, numerous paired gill-slits, and a branchial skeleton. Central nervous system closely connected with the skin, and heart dorsal to notochord. Mouth ventral, anus terminal. Body-cavity an enterocœle. Tornaria larva, presenting resemblances to Echinoderms, or Bateson's larva with posterior ciliated ring. Generally placed near the Echinoderms in a special group, *Enteropneusta*.

Cephalodiscus and **Rhabdopleura** are generally placed in the Polyzoa, as a sub-group *Pterobranchia*. Two gill-slits and a small notochord have been found in the former.

Subphylum B. **Urochorda** (Tunicata). Ascidians.

Marine hermaphrodites, usually of sac- or cask-shaped form. An external test of gelatinous or cartilaginous nature. Oral and atrial apertures. The first section of the gut is a pharynx perforated by gill-slits (branchial sac). Heart tubular and reversible. Asexual reproduction common, colonies being formed by budding.

In simple instances, *e.g. Ascidia*, the development shows great harmony with that of Amphioxus. After complete cleavage a gastrula is formed by embolic invagination. From the ectoderm a dorsal neural tube is developed, while a notochord (urochord) arises from the posterior part of the archenteron. The tailed larva exhibits metameric segmentation, but later on becomes an unsegmented animal by loss of the tail (with notochord), and reduction of the neural tube. In the Thaliacea there is a true alternation of generations (sexual and asexual generations alternate).

Order 1. *Larvacea* (Perennichordata, Copelatæ). Small free-swimming larva-like Ascidians ; the swimming tail persists, as also the nerve-cord, myotomes, and notochord (urochord). The anus and the two gill-slits open directly to the exterior.—A temporary gelatinous test secreted from time to time by the epidermis. **Appendicularia, Fritillaria.**

Order 2. *Ascidiæ* (Tethyodea, Caducichordata in part), sea squirts. A well-developed cartilaginous test and large pharynx perforated by numerous secondary gill-slits. Mostly sedentary.

A s c i d i æ s i m p l i c e s, oral and atrial apertures approximated: **Clavellina ; Ascidia mammillata ; Ciona intestinalis. Octacnemus bythius,** a deep-sea form.

A s c i d i æ c o m p o s i t æ, colonial forms with a common test ; individuals arranged in systems, each of which has a central cloacal cavity : **Botryllus.**

A s c i d i æ s a l p i f o r m e s ; free swimming colonies in the form of a hollow cylinder closed at one end ; the embryo develops into an asexual cyathozooid, which produces four sexual ascidiozooids by budding ; these constitute a new colony which continually enlarges by gemmation. **Pyrosoma,** phosphorescent.

Order 3. *Thaliacea* (Caducichordata in part), salps. Pelagic transparent ascidians. Oral and atrial apertures at opposite extremities. Development with alternation of generations, sexual individuals united in a chain.—**Salpa,** wall of pharynx reduced to a dorsal band (gill), **S. democratica** with **S. mucronata** as the chain-form. The egg develops to an embryo, which nourishes itself by a placenta in the brood-sac of the parent, and is born as a solitary asexual salp (nurse).—**Doliolum** with pharynx perforated by two transverse rows of gill-clefts and complicated alternation of generations.

Subphylum C. **Cephalochorda** (Pharyngobranchii, Acrania).

Marine Chordata with a continuous median fin but no paired fins. Axial skeleton represented by the notochord which extends from one end of the body to the other. No skull, jaws, true brain, sympathetic system, auditory organ, heart or spleen. An unpaired eye as a pigment-spot in the brain substance, and an unpaired olfactory pit. Blood colourless. Body-cavity an enterocœle. Excretory organs as a pair of short tubes opening into the atrial cavity surrounding the pharynx, this cavity opens to the exterior by an atriopore. Gonads arranged metamerically ; no gonaducts. Only one known genus. **Amphioxus lanceolatus,** lancelet.

K

Subphylum D. **Vertebrata** (Craniata).
Backboned Animals.

Chordata in which the notochord is supplemented, or more or less replaced, by a mesodermic axial skeleton consisting of a skull and segmented backbone. Never more than two pairs of limbs. Possess a distinct head which lodges a brain that extends in front of the notochord, two eyes with cup-shaped retina derived from the brain, two auditory vesicles with semicircular canals, and two olfactory pits. There is a heart with closed blood-system containing red as well as colourless corpuscles, and a subordinated lymphatic (and lacteal) system communicating with a large enterocœlic body-cavity. A spleen, and compact excretory organs opening by longitudinal ducts to the exterior always present. Gonads never arranged segmentally, ova usually pass into the body-cavity and thence into oviducts, and sperm carried off by excretory or special genital ducts. True hermaphrodites only found among fishes.

CRANIATA			
		No jaws or limbs, . . . **Cyclostomi.**	
	Persistent or temporary branchial respiration. Blood same temperature as surrounding medium. Without amnion and allantois. **Ichthyopsida** (Anamnia).	Jaws present. Two pairs of limbs.	Heart with auricle and ventricle. Median fin-rays. Branchial respiration. **Pisces.**
			Heart with two auricles and a ventricle. No median fin-rays. Lungs; temporary or persistent branchial respiration. A cloaca. **Amphibia.**
	Branchial respiration replaced by allantoic respiration in the embryo and pulmonary respiration in the adult. Possess an amnion. **Amniota.**	A single occipital condyle. Mandible articulates with a quadrate bone. A cloaca. Oviparous. **Sauropsida.**	Scales or scutes. Ventricle (usually) incompletely divided. Blood same temperature as surrounding medium. **Reptilia.**
			Feathers. Ventricle completely divided ; warm blooded. **Aves.**
		Two occipital condyles. Mandible articulates with skull. A respiratory diaphragm. Ventricle completely divided ; warm-blooded. Female with mammary glands. Viviparous, except the Monotremata. **Mammalia.**	

Class I. **Cyclostomi** (Marsipobranchii).

Eel-like forms without paired fins, with a rounded suctorial mouth not supported by jaws, an unconstricted notochord and cartilaginous skeleton, and six to seven pairs of branchial pouches. Nostril unpaired.

Order 1. *Hyperotreti.* The nasal passage communicates with the mouth-cavity.—**Myxine glutinosa,** hag.

Order 2. *Hyperoartia.* Nasal passage ends blindly.—**Petromyzon.** Larval form Ammocœtes. **P. Planeri; P. fluviatilis,** lampern; **P. marinus,** lamprey.

Class II. Pisces. Fishes.

Cold-blooded forms, with paired fins and median fin-rays, branchial respiration, and heart of one auricle and one ventricle. Mostly with scales.

Order 1. *Selachii* (Elasmobranchii, Plagiostomi). Cartilaginous fishes with placoid scales (dermal denticles), large pectoral and pelvic fins (the former tribasal), five pairs of gill-pouches (usually), a muscular conus arteriosus containing rows of valves, a spiral valve in the intestine, and a cloaca.

S q u a l i d æ (Selachoidei), sharks, with lateral gill-clefts. **Scyllium.** **Cestracion. Mustelus lævis** (smooth shark of Aristotle). **Acanthias vulgaris. Notidanus** (Heptanchus), seven pairs of gill-pouches. To these are appended the R a j i d æ (Batoidei), with ventral gill-clefts. **Pristis. Torpedo marmorata. Narcine. Raja clavata, R. batis.**

Order 2. *Holocephali.* Closely allied to Selachii, but skin naked, upper jaw fused to skull, notochord persistent, and four gill-clefts covered by a membranous operculum. No cloaca. **Chimæra. Callorhynchus.**

Order 3. *Ganoidei.* Cartilaginous and bony fishes with scales or scutes (ganoid scales), comb-shaped gills covered by a bony operculum, muscular conus arteriosus containing rows of valves, and a spiral valve in the intestine. No cloaca, but a urogenital aperture behind the anus. Numerous fossil, few recent forms.

C a r t i l a g i n o u s G a n o i d s, with persistent unconstricted notochord, heterocercal tail, spiracles and mandibular pseudobranchs. **Acipenser,** sturgeon, **Scaphirhynchus,** and **Polyodon** (Spatularia), recent. **Palæoniscus Freieslebeni,** Kupferschiefer. **Platysomus.**

B o n y G a n o i d s, with notochord constricted by vertebral centra, skull with membrane bones, and no mandibular pseudobranchs. **Polypterus bichir,** double swim-bladder, and **Calamoichthys,** recent. **Holoptychius,** Devonian. **Amia,** Cretaceous to recent, **A. calva,** recent. **Lepidosteus osseus,** bony pike, recent. **Pycnodus,** the unconstricted notochord surrounded by demi-vertebræ, Jurassic to Tertiary. **Lepidotus** and **Amblypterus** in the Kupferschiefer.

The armoured Ganoids **Coccosteus, Pterichthys,** and **Cephalaspis Lyellii** are peculiar extinct forms from the Devonian.

Order 4. *Teleostei.* Bony fishes with comb-like gills and (generally) a hyoidean pseudobranch, with bony operculum and two valves in the bulbus arteriosus. No optic chiasma, conus arteriosus, spiracles, or cloaca.

A. Physoklisti. Swim-bladder, when present, without pneumatic duct.

(*a.*) Lophobranchii. Exoskeleton of large dermal plates; gills tufted. **Pegasus; Syngnathus acus,** pipe-fish, and **Hippocampus,** sea-horse, male with brood-pouch in which the eggs are hatched.

(*b.*) Plectognathi. Compact forms with immovably fused premaxillæ and maxillæ; vertebral column short (18–20 vertebræ); a swim-bladder. **Ostracion,** box-fish; **Orthagoriscus mola,** sun-fish. **Diodon.**

(*c.*) Anacanthini, with soft fin-rays (Malacopteri); a swim-bladder. **Pleuronectidæ,** flat-fish. **Gadus morrhua,** cod, **G. æglefinus,** haddock, **G. merlangus,** whiting. **Fierasfer acus,** parasitic in Holothuria. **Exocœtus exiliens,** flying-fish.

(*d.*) Pharyngognathi, some of the fin-rays spinous; hypopharyngeal bones fused; a swim-bladder. **Labrus. Scarus. Embiotoca,** viviparous.

(*e.*) Acanthopteri, with spinous fin-rays, and separate hypopharyngeal bones; mostly ctenoid scales. **Perca fluviatilis,** perch. **Serranus scriba,** hermaphrodite. **Gasterosteus aculeatus,** stickleback; the male takes care of the young. **Cottus gobio,** bull-head. **Trigla,** gurnard. **Gobius,** gudgeon. **Zoarces viviparus. Mugil. Anabas scandens,** climbing fish (Labyrinthici).

B. Physostomi. Soft fin-rays and separate hypopharyngeal bones. Swim-bladder, when present, with a pneumatic duct. **Anguilla vulgaris,** eel; the male does not enter rivers. **Muræna, Gymnotus electricus. Clupea harengus,** herring. **Mormyrus** with pseudelectric organ. **Esox lucius,** pike. **Salmo salar,** salmon, with a fatty fin. **Cyprinus carpio,** carp. **Cobitis fossilis,** loach. **Silurus. Malapterurus electricus,** sheat-fish.

Order 5. *Dipnoi*, mud fishes ; lead on to the Amphibians. With persistent notochord, paired limbs supported by a central jointed axis, branchial and pulmonary respiration, muscular conus arteriosus, spiral valve to the intestine, and a cloaca.

M o n o p n e u m o n a, with a single lung ; Trias to recent. **Ceratodus Forsteri,** Queensland.

D i p n e u m o n a, paired lungs. **Protopterus annectens,** W. Africa (with three pairs of branched external gills). **Lepidosiren paradoxa,** Brazil.

Class III. Amphibia.

Cold-blooded Vertebrates with naked glandular skin, a sacral vertebra, and (generally) paired limbs, consisting of girdle with free limb transversely divided into three regions.· A cloaca, lungs, temporary or permanent branchial respiration, and an incomplete double circulation. Median fins, when present, not supported by fin-rays. Amnion absent, and allantois represented by a urinary bladder. Frequently a metamorphosis.

Order 1. *Urodela* (Caudata), tailed forms.

I c h t h y o i d e a, notochord largely persistent, and vertebræ biconcave : **Proteus anguineus,** in the underground streams of Carniola ; **Siredon pisciformis,** Axolotl, may lose its gills (becoming Amblystoma); both preceding perennibranch. **Menopoma,** and **Sieboldia** (Cryptobranchus) **Japonicus,** lose their gills (caducibranch), but retain a pair of gill-clefts.

S a l a m a n d r i n a (Myctodera), adults without gills or gill-clefts; vertebræ opisthocœlous. **Triton cristatus,** great water newt, with spermatheca, oviparous. **Salamandra maculosa,** viviparous.

Order 2. *Batrachia* (Anura). With elongated hind-limbs, and 9–11 procœlous vertebræ. Tail, gills, and gill-slits only present in the larva. **Pipa dorsigera,** female with brood-pouches on the back. **Rana esculenta,** edible frog, **R. temporaria,** common frog, **R. oxyrhinus. Bombinator igneus. Bufo vulgaris,** toad. **Hyla arborea,** tree-frog, toes with suckers.

Order 3. *Apoda* (Gymnophiona). Serpent-shaped subterranean forms devoid of limbs, tail, gills, and gill-clefts. Skin with small dermal scales ; vertebræ amphicœlous. **Cœcilia lumbricoidea. Epicrium. Siphonops.**

Order 4. *Stegocephali.* Extinct forms, often of large size, with tail, dermal armour, and well-ossified pubes. Carboniferous to Trias. **Labyrinthodon.**

Class IV. **Reptilia.**

Cold-blooded Vertebrates breathing by lungs, and possessing scales or scutes. A single occipital condyle, generally two sacral vertebræ, and (in recent forms) ischial and pubic symphyses and separate pelvic bones and metatarsals. Heart with two auricles and either an imperfectly divided ventricle or perfectly divided one with mixture of blood-streams outside heart; at least two aortic arches.

The following groups of Reptiles covered with scales or scutes are grouped together as L e p i d o s a u r i a (Plagiotremata).

Order 1. *Lacertilia* (Sauria), lizards. Cloacal aperture a transverse slit; a urinary bladder and two eversible copulatory organs. **Protero-saurus** (Upper Dyas). **Telerpeton** (biconcave vertebræ, Trias).—**Gecko** and **Platydactylus** with biconcave vertebræ. **Iguana. Draco volans. Chamæleo vulgaris.**—**Scincus. Pseudopus Pallassii** and **Anguis fragilis,** blindworm, limbless.—**Lacerta agilis, L. vivipara. Monitor varanus. Mosasaurus** (Chalk).—**Amphisbæna. Hatteria** (Spheno-don), biconcave vertebræ, no copulatory organs.

Order 2. *Pterosauria,* Lias to Chalk. Antebrachium and fifth digit of manus greatly elongated. Jaws usually dentigerous. Bones pneumatic. **Pterodactylus longirostris. Pteranodon,** toothless.

Order 3. *Ophidia,* snakes. Limbless, and without urinary bladder. Jaw apparatus with elastic bands. **Typhlops,** mouth cannot be widely opened.

C o l u b r i f o r m i a: **Boa constrictor. Python. Coronella aus-triaca** (=lævis) smooth viper. **Tropidonotus natrix,** common snake. **Coluber. Dryophis.**

P r o t e r o g l y p h a, poisonous snakes, with grooved fangs in the front of the upper jaw : **Naja tripudians,** cobra. **Hydrophis,** Indian Ocean.

S o l e n o g l y p h i a, with triangular head, and a poison-fang on either side of the small upper jaw. **Pelias** (Vipera) **berus,** adder. **Crotalus horridus,** rattlesnake.

The following two groups are included under the name of H y d r o-s a u r i a (large aquatic forms with teeth firmly implanted in the jaw, feet·modified for swimming and strong or armoured skin).

Order 4. *Enaliosauria*, with naked leathery skin, paddles, and biconcave vertebræ (all from the Secondary period).—**Nothosaurus.** **Plesiosaurus dolichodeirus.**—**Ichthyosaurus communis.**

Order 5. *Crocodilia*, with a long tail, webbed feet, scales, and scutes. Teeth in sockets, ventricle completely divided, longitudinal cloacal aperture and solid grooved penis.—**Teleosaurus**, Jurassic, amphicœlous vertebræ.—**Steneosaurus**, Jurassic and Cretaceous, vertebræ opisthocœlous.—Procœlous vertebræ from the Cretaceous on : **Alligator lucius** and **Caiman** in America, **Crocodilus vulgaris** in the Nile. **Gavialis gangeticus.**

Order 6. *Chelonia*, with bony dorsal and ventral dermal shields ; edentulous ; a urinary bladder and solid grooved penis. **Chelone midas,** edible turtle. **Trionyx.** **Cistudo** (Emys) **Europæa, Emys caspica. Testudo Græca,** land tortoise.

Order 7. *Dinosauria.* Fossil forms which possessed more than two sacral vertebræ, and were in many respects, especially as regards the pelvis and hind limb, intermediate between Reptiles and Birds. **Iguanodon. Megalosaurus Bucklandi** (Jurassic and Wealden).—Also **Dicynodon** in the Trias.

M

Class V. **Aves.** Birds.

Feathered warm-blooded vertebrates with lungs closely adherent to the back of the thorax and communicating with air-sacs which extend between the viscera and into the bones. Ventricle completely divided, the right auriculo-ventricular valve muscular, and a single aortic arch curving to the right. Occipital region with a single condyle, numerous vertebræ fused to form a pseud-sacrum, fore-limbs wings, pelvis with fused bones, and (as a rule) neither pubic nor ischial symphyses, ankle-joint between a tibio-tarsus and tarso-metatarsus. Right ovary and oviduct rudimentary ; oviparous. Some toothed fossil forms.

Order 1. *Saururæ*. Numerous free caudal vertebræ ; jaws with teeth. **Archæopteryx lithographica** from the Upper Oolite.

Order 2. *Ratitæ* (Cursores). Wings rudimentary, no keel to the sternum.

Dinornis, extinct moa of New Zealand. **Struthio camelus**, ostrich, Deserts of N., E., and S. Africa, Arabia, and Syria. **Rhea Americana**, S. America. **Dromæus**, emeu, Australia. **Casuarius**, cassowary, New Guinea, &c., and N. Australia. **Apteryx australis**, with complete diaphragm and air-sacs situated in the thorax; New Zealand. O d o n t o l c æ, with teeth in grooves. **Hesperornis**, from the Cretaceous.

Order 3. *Carinatæ.* Wings well developed, sternum with a keel.

Odontormæ, biconcave vertebræ, teeth in sockets. **Ichthyornis** from the Cretaceous.

Urinatores, wings short, sickle-shaped. **Aptenodytes. Podiceps. Alca impennis,** exterminated.

Longipennes, beak hooked. **Diomedea exulans,** albatross. **Procellaria Larus.**

Steganopodes, with webbed feet. **Pelecanus onocrotalus.**

Lamellirostres, edges of the beak with horny plates. **Cygnus olor. Anser. Anas boschas.**

Grallæ, palate schizognathous. **Scolopax. Grus cinerea.**

Ciconiæ, **Ardea cinerea. Ciconia alba. Ibis rubra.** Otis **tarda.**

Rasores, gallinaceous birds. **Tetrao. Perdix. Gallus bankiva. Pavo.**

Columbæ (Gyrantes), doves. **Columba livia. Didus ineptus,** exterminated.

Raptores, birds of prey. **Strix. Vultur. Falco. Aquila.**

Passeres, special muscle to the syrinx. **Fringilla cœlebs. Alauda. Hirundo. Sturnus. Corvus. Paradisea.**

Macrochires. **Caprimulgus. Cypselus apus. Trochilus colubris.**

Pici, tongue slender and extensible. **Picus.**

Levirostres (Coccygomorphæ) palate desmognathous. **Cuculus canorus. Buceros. Upupa epops.**

Psittaci, upper jaw hinged on the skull. **Psittacus erithacus. Nestor. Strigops,** no keel to sternum.

Class VI. Mammalia.

Hair-clothed, warm-blooded vertebrates, viviparous with the exception of Monotremes; milk-glands always present in the female. A double circulation, membranous right auriculo-ventricular valve, single aortic arch curving to the left, and non-nucleated red blood-corpuscles. A complete muscular diaphragm (respiratory muscle). Two occipital condyles, and seven (6–9) cervical vertebræ.

Sub-Class I. PROTOTHERIA (Ornithodelphia).

Order 1. *Monotremata.* A persistent cloaca, epipubic (marsupial) bones and beak-like horny jaws. Oviparous. Ova large and cleavage meroblastic. No placenta. Only three genera are known. **Ornithorhynchus**, duck-billed platypus, Australia and Tasmania; **Echidna** (Tachyglossus), and **Proechidna** (Acanthoglossus), spiny ant-eaters, the former in Australia, Tasmania, and North New Guinea, the latter in South New Guinea.

Sub-Class II. METATHERIA (Didelphia, Implacentalia).

Order 1. *Marsupialia*, pouched animals. Epipubic (marsupial) bones; in the female, two uteri, usually two vaginæ and a marsupial pouch, genital aperture and anus surrounded by a common sphincter; in the male, scrotum suspended in front of the penis. Auditory bulla formed by alisphenoid, angle of the lower jaw inflected. Generally very numerous teeth, which (with a few exceptions) are not changed; incisors never $\frac{3-3}{3-3}$. No allantoic placenta (so far as known).

(*a.*) R a p a c i a, carnivorous marsupials. **Perameles,** $\frac{5(4)}{3} \frac{1}{1} \frac{3}{3} \left| \frac{4}{4} \right.$.

Myrmecobius, $\frac{4}{3} \frac{1}{1} \frac{4}{4} \frac{5}{5}$. **Dasyurus viverrinus,** dasyure. **Thylacinus,** native wolf. **Thylacoleo,** Pleistocene.

(*b.*) P e d i m a n a, opossums. Dentition carnivorous, and resembling that of the Insectivora, $\frac{5}{4} \frac{1}{1} \frac{3}{3} \left| \frac{4}{4} \right.$. **Didelphys Americana,** American opossum; as many as twenty-seven young at a birth. **Chironectes.**

(*c.*) C a r p o p h a g a, frugivorous marsupials with corresponding dentition. **Phalangista vulpina,** phalanger. **Petaurus. Phascolarctos,** $\frac{3}{1} \frac{1}{0} \frac{1}{1} \left| \frac{4}{4} \right.$.

(*d.*) P o ë p h a g a (Macropoda), springing marsupials. The two lower incisors horizontal; dentition $\frac{3}{1} \frac{0(1)}{0} \frac{1}{1} \left| \frac{4}{4} \right.$. **Microlestes** from the Trias. **Diprotodon australis** in the Pleistocene. **Macropus** (Halmaturus) **gigantea,** kangaroo.

(*e.*) G l i r i n a (Rhizophaga), gnawing marsupials. **Phascolomys** wombat $\frac{1}{1} \frac{0}{0} \frac{1}{1} \left| \frac{4}{4} \right.$.

N

Sub-Class III. EUTHERIA (Monodelphia, Placentalia).

The embryo is nourished by means of an allantoic placenta ; the marsupium and epipubic bones are absent ; vagina single ; scrotum, when present, behind the penis. Alisphenoid does not form an auditory bulla ; angle of mandible rarely inflected.

Fossil from the Eocene onwards.

A. *NON-DECIDUATA.*   Placenta non-deciduate (except in some Edentates).

Order 1. *Edentata* (Bruta).   Teeth of persistent growth and without enamel ; median incisors never present; grinding teeth, when present, similar and rootless.

(*a.*) Phytophaga, arboreal vegetable-feeding South American forms, with dome-shaped deciduate placenta.   **Bradypus,** three-toed sloth, with tridactyle manus and nine cervical vertebræ.   **Cholœpus,** two-toed sloth, with didactyle manus and six to seven cervical vertebræ.   **Megatherium** and **Mylodon,** gigantic ground sloths, from the South American Pleistocene.

(*b.*) Entomophaga, insectivorous forms.   **Myrmecophaga,** great ant-eater (S. America), and **Manis,** pangolin or scaly ant-eater (E. Africa and S. Asia), both toothless, the former with a dome-shaped deciduate, the latter with a diffuse placenta.—**Orycteropus,** aard-vark (S. Africa), with zonary deciduate placenta.—**Dasypus** and **Chlamydophorus,** armadilloes (S. America) with bony dermal plates covered by epidermic scales, and discoidal deciduate placenta.   **Glyptodon,** a large armadillo from the S. American Pleistocene.

Order 2. *Ungulata.* Hoofed mammals, with elongated metacarpals and metatarsals, and two successive sets of enamel-covered teeth. Clavicles never present; never more than four digits.

(*a.*) Artiodactyla, paired digits, and grinding teeth with enamel folds. Placenta diffuse or cotyledonary.

Non-ruminantia (Bunodontia). **Anthracotherium,** a primæval form from the Eocene. **Porcus babyrussa. Sus scrofa,** pig, $\dfrac{3}{3}\ \dfrac{1}{1}\ \dfrac{4}{4}\ \Big|\ \dfrac{3}{3}$. Sus antiquus, Miocene. **Hippopotamus amphibius.**

Ruminantia (Bisulca, Pecora, Selenodontia), with complicated stomach; median upper incisors always absent. **Anoplotherium,** Miocene. **Camelus. Auchenia,** llama. **Helladotherium** and **Sivatherium,** Miocene. **Camelopardalis giraffus. Dorcatherium,** Miocene. **Tragulus,** chevrotain, recent. **Megaceros Hibernicus,** Irish elk, Pleistocene. **Cervus capreolus,** roe, **C. elaphus,** red deer, **C. alces,** elk. **Capra. Ovis. Bos primigenius, B. brachyceros, B. frontosus.**

(*b.*) Perissodactyla, a large middle digit (3rd) symmetrical in itself, and pes with an odd number of toes. Placenta diffuse. **Lophiodon, Palæotherium,** and **Eohippus,** in the Eocene. **Tapirus,** S. America and S.E. Asia. **Rhinoceros,** S. Africa and S. Asia. **Equus.**

Order 3. *Cetacea.* Marine (rarely fluviatile or estuarine) Mammals, of fish-like form, with almost hairless skin, paddle-like fore-limbs without nails, and horizontally flattened tail-fin. No hind-limbs, clavicles, or distinct sacrum. Teeth, when present in adult, numerous, similar, and without vertical successors. Placenta diffuse.

(*a.*) Denticeti, toothed Cetaceans; **Zeuglodon** (Tertiary). **Delphinus delphis**, dolphin. **Phocæna communis**, porpoise. **Monodon**, narwhal. **Physeter tursio**.

(*b*) Mysticeti, right whales. **Balænoptera rostrata. Balæna Mysticetus.**

Order 4. *Sirenia,* sea-cows. Aquatic Mammals with scanty hair, paddle-like fore-limbs with rudimentary nails, and horizontally flattened tail-fin. No hind-limbs, clavicles, or sacrum. Dentition herbivorous. Placenta diffuse.—**Manatus**, manatee (E. coast of S. America and W. coast of Africa), with six cervical vertebræ. **Halicore**, dugong (shores of Indian Ocean and Red Sea). **Rhytina Stelleri**, exterminated last century. **Halitherium**, Pliocene.

B. *DECIDUATA.* Placenta deciduate (except in the Prosimiæ).

Order 5. *Rodentia* (Glires). Mammals with (usually) five clawed digits to the manus and pes, $\frac{1}{1}$ chisel-shaped continuously growing incisors, and 3–6 back teeth with transverse folds of enamel; no canines. Placenta discoidal.—**Lepus timidus,** hare. **L. cuniculus,** rabbit. **Cavia cobaya, C. aperea,** guinea-pig. **Hydrochœrus capybara, Hystrix,** porcupine. **Pedetes caffer,** Cape jumping hare. **Cricetus frumentarius,** hamster. **Mus rattus,** black rat. **M. decumanus,** brown rat. **M. musculus,** mouse. **Arvicola,** vole. **Myodes,** lemming. **Castor fiber,** beaver. **Myoxus,** dormouse. **Sciurus vulgaris,** squirrel.

o

Order 6. *Proboscidea.* Pentadactyle hoofed Mammalia with prehensile proboscis, two tusk-like continuously growing upper incisors, no canines, and composite grinding teeth. Placenta zonary. **Mastodon**, Miocene to Pleistocene. **Deinotherium**, with two tusk-like *lower* incisors. Miocene. **Elephas primigenius**, mammoth, Pleistocene,—**E.** (Euelephas) **Indicus**, Indian elephant, S. Asia,—**E.** (Loxodon) **Africanus**, African elephant, Africa S. of the Sahara.

Order 7. *Hyracoidea* (Lamnugia), conies. Small rodent-like Mammals with pentadactyle (but two digits rudimentary) manus and tridactyle pes. Dental formula $\dfrac{2}{2}\ \dfrac{0}{0}\ \dfrac{4}{4}\ \bigg|\ \dfrac{3}{3}$, upper outer incisors soon fall out, upper median incisors chisel-like, and continuously growing. Placenta zonary.—**Hyrax,** Africa and Syria.

Order 8. *Insectivora.* Small pentadactyle plantigrade or sub-plantigrade Mammals, with clawed digits and (almost always) clavicles. Always more than two lower incisors, canines small, molars with fangs and sharply pointed crowns. Placenta discoidal.—**Erinaceus Europæus,** hedgehog. **Sorex,** shrew. **Talpa,** mole.

Order 9. *Cheiroptera,* bats. Mammals in which there is a flying membrane (patagium) stretched between the body, limbs, and elongated digits of the manus. Dentition complete, incisors smaller than the canines. Clavicles well developed, sternum keeled, mammæ pectoral. Placenta discoidal.

(*a.*) Frugivora (Megacheiroptera), fruit-eating forms; **Pteropus edulis.**

(*b.*) Insectivora (Microcheiroptera), insectivorous or blood-sucking forms; **Vespertilio. Plecotus. Vampyrus.**

Order 10. *Carnivora* (Feræ), beasts of prey. Pentadactyle clawed Mammals, with complete dentition. Incisors generally $\frac{3}{3}$, canines strong. Clavicles absent or rudimentary. Placenta zonary.

(*a*) Fissipedia; terrestrial forms with well-developed claws, and extremities seldom webbed. Incisors $\frac{3}{3}$, canines long and pointed, præmolars (*dentes spurii*) pointed, molars mostly small and irregular; the last upper præmolars and first lower molars are large rending teeth (carnassial or sectorial). **Ursus,** p.m. $\frac{4}{4}$ m. $\frac{2}{3}$. **Mustela martes,** martin, p.m. $\frac{4}{4}$ m. $\frac{1}{2}$. **Viverra,** p.m. $\frac{4}{4}$ m. $\frac{2}{2}$. **Canis,** p.m. $\frac{4}{4}$ m. $\frac{2}{3(2)}$. **Hyæna,** p.m. $\frac{4}{3}$ m. $\frac{1}{1}$. **Felis,** p.m. $\frac{3}{2}$ m. $\frac{1}{1}$.

(*b*) Pinnipedia; aquatic forms with rudimentary claws and webbed extremities; the hind-limbs united with the tail by a fold of skin. Grinding teeth all similar, and never with more than two fangs. **Phoca vitulina,** common seal, i. $\frac{3}{2}$ c. $\frac{1}{1}$ p.m. + m. $\frac{5}{5}$. **Otaria,** sea lion or eared seal. **Trichechus rosmarus,** walrus.

Order 11. *Prosimiæ* (Lemuroidea), lemurs. Quadrupedal Mammals with prehensile extremities, opposable hallux, and long non-prehensile tail. Hallux (and generally pollex) with a flat nail, remaining digits clawed. Orbits incompletely separated from the temporal fossæ. Uterus bicornuate, clitoris perforated by urethra, mammæ pectoral and abdominal, placenta diffuse.

(*a*.) Cheiromyini ; **Cheiromys Madagascarensis**, pollex non-opposable and clawed ; i. $\frac{1}{1}$ c. $\frac{0}{0}$ p.m. $+$ m. $\frac{4}{3}$.

(*b*.) Lemurini, with large opposable flat-nailed pollex ; lower incisors forwardly directed. Limited to S. Africa and S. Asia ; **Tarsius**, dentition $\frac{2}{1}$ $\frac{1}{1}$ $\frac{3}{3}$ $\Big|$ $\frac{3}{3}$. **Lemur**, $\frac{2}{2}$ $\frac{1}{1}$ $\frac{3}{3}$ $\Big|$ $\frac{3}{3}$.

Order 12. *Primates.* Hallux (and generally pollex) with a flat nail and relatively short. Orbits completely or almost completely separated from temporal fossæ. Uterus simple, clitoris not perforated by urethra, a pair of pectoral mammæ, placenta metadiscoidal.

(*a*.) Arctopitheci, marmozets (S. America) ; quadrupedal, long non-prehensile tail, and non-opposable clawed pollex. Orbits not quite walled off from temporal fossæ. Dental formula $\frac{2}{2}$ $\frac{1}{1}$ $\frac{3}{3}$ $\Big|$ $\frac{2}{2}$. **Hapale**.

(*b*.) Platyrrhini, New World monkeys ; quadrupedal, long generally prehensile tail, non-opposable pollex, nailed digits, and broad nasal septum. Orbits completely separated from temporal fossæ, coronal suture V-shaped, alisphenoids united with parietals, external auditory meatus not ossified. Dental formula $\frac{2}{2}$ $\frac{1}{1}$ $\frac{3}{3}$ $\Big|$ $\frac{3}{3}$. Neither cheek-pouches nor ischial callosities. **Cebus capucinus**. **Mycetes niger**, howling monkey. **Pithecia satanas**.

(*c*) Catarrhini, Old World monkeys. Tail, when present, non-prehensile, opposable pollex, nailed digits, and narrow nasal septum. Orbits completely separated from temporal fossæ, alisphenoids not united with parietals, external auditory meatus ossified. Dental formula $\frac{2}{2}$ $\frac{1}{1}$ $\frac{2}{2}$ $\Big|$ $\frac{3}{3}$. C y n o m o r p h a, baboons, &c.; quadrupedal tailed forms, with ischial callosities, and, as a rule, cheek-pouches. **Cynocephalus**. **Macacus**. **Cercopithecus sabæus**. A n t h r o p o m o r p h a, arboreal semi-erect tailless forms. **Hylobates**, gibbon (S. E. Asia and Malay Archipelago), with ischial callosities. **Pithecus** (Satyrus), orang (Borneo and Sumatra), 12 pairs of ribs. **Gorilla engena** (Troglodytes gorilla) and **Troglodytes niger**, chimpanzee, both from W. Africa, and with 13 pairs of ribs.

(*d*) Anthropidæ, distinguished from the other groups of Primates by the following characters :—Hair scanty, position habitually erect, hallux non-opposable, cranio-facial angle not greater than 120°, mandibular symphysis with a mental prominence, no diastema in the dental series, volume of brain not less than 55 cubic inches. **Homo sapiens**, man.

P

PRINCIPLES OF DISTRIBUTION.

Explanatory Theories—

I. *Theory of Special Creations*, now abandoned. According to it:—1. Organisms were created where now found. 2. The fauna and flora of any particular region must be better adapted to it than any other fauna and flora. 3. Climate, soil, and position explain all the phenomena of distribution.

II. *Theory of Evolution*, generally accepted. Regards modern distribution as the result of innumerable changes that have affected—(1) organisms ; (2) the surface of the globe.

1. Geological history shows that there has been a succession of faunas and floras passing gradually into one another, old species becoming extinct, and new ones being evolved by the combined influence of variation and heredity, which respectively originate and accumulate new characters. Upon the whole a gradual advance in complexity has taken place, but the geological record is extremely imperfect, especially as regards land organisms. The process of change is still going on, and examples of modern extinction (*e.g.* the New Zealand **Dinornis** and Sirenian form **Rhytina**) are well known, but the detection of newly evolved species involves greater difficulties.

Species once established have extended themselves over smaller or larger areas, according to their powers of migration and surrounding conditions, *i.e.*, their environment. Physical barriers, such as oceans, mountains, climate, and soil, have played an important part in limiting such extension, but the competition of other forms has had a still greater influence. Introduced forms often increase prodigiously, and even supersede the indigenous ones, whence it follows that these last are not necessarily the best adapted. *Exs.* Rabbits in Australia ; the brown rat in England, which has almost ousted the indigenous black rat.

2. Owing to the wearing away or erosion of the land by various agencies (chiefly the different forms of water), and the action of subterranean forces by which upward and downward movements of the earth's crust are produced, the distribution of land and sea has constantly varied. Europe and North America, for example, have most likely been connected at various times by land occupying part of what is now the North Atlantic, and Australia appears to have been once united with Asia. On the other hand, evidence is found on every continental land surface of the former presence of the sea. In spite of what has been said, the theory of "permanence of oceanic and continental areas" finds much support. According to it the great oceans are of extreme antiquity, and, *on the whole*, more or less land has existed from very remote times within the present continental areas. It is perhaps best to accept this theory only for the deeper parts of the great oceans. An accurate knowledge of the contours of the ocean-floor is important in this connection, and serves as an important check upon speculations regarding former land-unions. On this basis islands have been divided into *oceanic* and *continental*, which are believed respectively to have been always isolated, and to have been connected with an adjoining continent.

Oceanic Islands are :—(a) generally remote from continents ; (b) separated from them by very deep (usually over 1000 fathoms) water ; (c) of volcanic or coral nature ; (d) inhabited by forms which possess powers of migration capable of carrying them, actively or passively, over more or less broad ocean tracts ; (e) characterised by numerous peculiar species. *Exs.* The Azores, St. Helena, Ascension, coral islands of Pacific.

Continental islands are:—(a) comparatively near a continent ; (b) separated from it by comparatively shallow (under 1000 fathoms) water ; (c) of similar geological structure, and not entirely volcanic or coral ; (d) inhabited by similar organisms, irrespective of powers of migration. Such islands are :—(1) *Ancient continental*, separated from the nearest continent by fairly deep (over 1000 fathoms) water, and presenting only a general resemblance in the fauna and flora ; many peculiar species. *Exs.* Madagascar, Malay Islands. (2) *Recent continental*, separated from the adjacent continent by shallow (not more than 100 fathoms) water, and with closely similar fauna and flora ; very few peculiar species. *Exs.* British Islands, Japan. Both (1) and (2) have presumably been united with the adjoining continents, the latter at a recent date, geologically speaking.

The surface of the globe has also undergone numerous mutations as regards *climate*. The temperate parts of N. America and Europe, for example, were at a geologically recent period passing through a glacial epoch (the "great ice age"), as proved by ice-worn and scratched rock-surfaces and rocks, boulder-clay, &c. On the other hand, fossil plants evidencing subtropical conditions have been found in the Arctic regions. Many

theories have been advanced to account for secular changes of climate. The most satisfactory is one by Wallace which attributes them to geographical revolutions (previously suggested by Lyell), influenced by astronomical changes (variations in excentricity of earth's orbit and movements of precession, as advanced by Croll).

All the preceding changes must have exerted a profound influence upon organisms, and throw light upon many problems of distribution.

Areas of Distribution.—May be mapped out for species genera, families, and orders. In all cases: (1) Size and nature of boundaries very variable. (2) Need not be continuous.

(a.) *Exs. of Limited Areas.*—The marmot only found in the Alps. A species of humming-bird confined to the crater of the extinct volcano Chiriqui in Veragua.

Six genera of Lemurs are peculiar to Madagascar. The family *Galeopithecidæ* (including the single genus **Galeopithecus**) is limited to Malacca, Sumatra, Borneo, and the Philippines. The order *Monotremata* only occurs in Australia, Tasmania, and New Guinea.

(b.), *Exs. of Extensive Areas.*—The leopard is distributed through the whole of Africa and S. Asia to Borneo and E. China. The genus **Felis** (cat, lion, leopard, &c.) ranges over most of the globe except Australia, the Pacific Islands, W. Indies, Madagascar, and the more northerly parts of N. America and Asia. The family *Vespertilionidæ*, including 200 species of small insect-eating bats, occurs everywhere within the tropical and temperate zones; while the family *Muridæ* (rats, mice, &c.) is only absent from Polynesia and New Zealand. 2. Discontinuity is generally a sign of antiquity, the two or more parts being remains of a once continuous distributional area, in part of which extinction has occurred. Changes in the distribution of land and sea have broken up many once continuous areas. *Examples.*—The variable hare (**Lepus variabilis**), Europe and Asia N. of 55°; Alps, Pyrenees, and Caucasus. The genus **Tapirus**, S. America, S. E. Asia. *Centetidæ* (a family of the Insectivora), Madagascar, Cuba, Hayti.

Ganoid fishes are now represented by genera with the following distribution:—
Acipenser, N. temperate and Arctic regions. Most species marine, others are found in the Caspian Sea, Black Sea, and N. American lakes, with their rivers, also in the Danube, Mississippi, and Columbia. **Scaphirhynchus**, Mississippi and tributaries. **Polyodon**, Mississippi, and Yang-tse-Kiang. **Polypterus**, Nile and W. African rivers. **Calamoichthys**, rivers of Old Calabar. **Amia**, fresh-water, United States. **Lepidosteus**, fresh-water, N. America to Mexico and Cuba. Ganoid fishes are of great geological antiquity, and were formerly a widely spread *marine* group. Most of the forms now surviving have gradually accommodated themselves to a life in rivers, lakes, &c., where the struggle for existence is less severe.

The peculiar distribution of the *Dipnoi* (p. 161) can be explained similarly.

The *Marsupialia* and *Edentata* (p. 235) are also good examples of interrupted areas of distribution.

Zoological Regions, characterised by the presence of peculiar families and genera, and by the absence of other families and genera, have been formed for sea and land. The most useful division of the latter is chiefly based on the Mammalia, but applies very well to birds and reptiles and fairly to other groups. The regions thus established are six in number.

I. *Palæarctic Region.*—Temperate Europe and Asia and N. temperate Africa. Extends W. to Iceland, the Azores, and Cape Verde Islands, and E. to Behring Straits and Japan. Southern boundary somewhat indefinite,—tropic of Cancer in Africa and Arabia, river Indus, Himalayas, Nanling mountains.

II. *Ethiopian Region.*—Africa and Arabia S. of the tropic of Cancer, and including Madagascar.

III. *Oriental Region.*—Asia, S. of Region I., and the western part of the E. Indies. The E. boundary of this region (*Wallace's line*) passes between Bali, Borneo, and the Philippines on the one hand, Lombok and Celebes on the other. The former islands are therefore in the Oriental Region, the latter in the Australian Region.

IV. *Australian Region.*—Australia, New Guinea, New Zealand, with the smaller islands from Wallace's line to the Marquesas and Low Archipelago, and the tropic of Cancer to the Macquarie Islands.

V. *Neotropical Region.*—S. America, the W. Indies, and tropical N. America, with the exception of the central part of the Mexican table-land.

VI. *Nearctic Region.*—Arctic and temperate N. America, with the central part of the Mexican table-land.

DISTRIBUTION OF MAMMALS.

I. *Palæarctic Region.*—Thirty-five families represented. *Peculiar Genera.* The camels, six deer, the yak, six antelopes (including the chamois), and all wild sheep and goats, except two species. Six p.g. of *Muridæ* (rats and mice), two of mole-rats, and one other; dormice and pikas (calling hares) are almost confined to this region. Six p.g. of moles; the remaining two genera of which (**Talpa, Urotrichus**) extend, respectively, into N. India and N. W. America. Five p.g. of Carnivora, including the racoon-dog, a seal, and the badger; the last just enters the Oriental region in China.

II. *Ethiopian Region.*—Fifty families represented, of which nine are peculiar, *i.e. Orycteropodidæ. Hippopotamidæ ; Camelopardidæ. Potamogalidæ* (including **Potamogale**, an otter-like Insectivore); *Chrysochloridæ* (golden moles). *Cryptoproctidæ* (**Cryptoprocta** is a small civet-cat-like form peculiar to Madagascar); *Protelidæ* (**Proteles**, the aard-wolf, is allied to the hyænas and weasels); *Cheiromyidæ* (contains **Cheiromy**, the aye-aye, peculiar to Madagascar).

Peculiar Genera (besides those in the above families).—**Potamochærus** (river hog), and **Phacochærus** (wart hog); **Hyomoschus** (a small deer-like form), twelve p.g. of antelopes. Thirteen p.g. of *Muridæ ;* **Pedetes** (a jerboa or jumping mouse); **Anomalurus** (a flying squirrel); three other p.g. of Rodenta. Three p.g. of elephant-shrews, and the Insectivorous family *Centetidæ*, except one genus from Cuba and Haytl. Three p.g. of bats. Seventeen p.g. of *Viverridæ* (civets and ichneumons), two p.g. of dogs, and two p.g. of *Mustelidæ* (weasels, otters, &c.). Nine p.g. of Lemurs. Eight p.g. of apes and monkeys, the most important being **Gorilla** and **Troglodytes** (chimpanzee).

Peculiar Species.—Among these are several species of Manis, the two-horned African rhinoceroses, the zebras, African elephant, and lion.

Absent Palæarctic Forms.—The genera **Bos** (wild ox), and **Sus** (wild boar), camels, deer, goats and sheep, moles, bears.

III. *Oriental Region.*—Forty-two families represented, of which two are peculiar, and one other almost so, *i.e., Galeopithecidæ* (including **Galeopithecus**, the flying lemur), and *Tupaiidæ* (tree-shrews), among Insectivora. *Tarsiidæ*, a family of lemurs (including only **Tarsius spectrum**, found in Sumatra, Banca, and Borneo ; also outside the Oriental region in Celebes.)

Peculiar Genera (besides those in the above families).—**Tragulus** (chevrotain) ; **Cervulus** (a deer) ; **Bibos** (wild cattle) ; three p.g. of antelopes. **Platanista** (a dolphin found in Ganges and Indus). Three p.g. of *Muridæ ;* **Pteromys** (a flying squirrel ; **Acanthion** (a porcupine). **Gymnura** (a hedgehog). Eleven p.g. of bats. Twelve p.g. of *Viverridæ ;* **Cuon** (a dog) ; five p.g. of *Mustelidæ ;* two p.g. of bears. **Loris** and **Nycticebus** (lemurs). Four p.g. of apes, including **Pithecus** (orang-utan), and **Hylobates** (gibbon).

Peculiar Species.—Among these are the Indian tapir, several species of rhinoceros, and the Indian elephant.

IV. *Australian Region.*—Twenty-eight families represented, of which eight are peculiar, *i.e.* six out of the seven families of Marsupials, and the two families of Monotremes. All of these, however, are absent from Polynesia and New Zealand.

Peculiar Genera (besides those in the above families).—**Babirusa** (a hog) and **Anoa** (a small kind of cow) in Celebes. Five p.g. of *Muridæ* in Australia, and one of these in Tasmania also. Three p.g. of bats.

Absent Forms.—Australia and New Guinea possess no non-aquatic Mammals higher than Marsupials, except some bats, mice, and rats. This points to extremely long-continued isolation, which has afforded time for the Marsupials to become modified in the most diverse directions, thus enabling them to fill places elsewhere occupied by other orders. New Zealand is remarkable for the absence of all indigenous Mammals, so far as certainly known, with the exception of two bats.

V. *Neotropical Region.*—Thirty-seven families represented, of which seven are peculiar, *i.e. Bradypodidæ* (sloths), *Dasypodidæ* (armadilloes), and *Myrmecophagidæ* (true ant-eaters). *Chinchillidæ* (chinchillas) and *Caviidæ* (cavies) among Rodents. *Cebidæ* (New World monkeys) ; *Hapalidæ* (marmozets). The *Phyllostomidæ* (leaf-nosed bats) are peculiar with the exception of a Californian species.

Peculiar Genera (besides those in the above families). **Chironectes** and **Hyracodon** (opossums). **Dicotyles** (peccary, also in Texas) ; **Auchenia** (llama); **Elasmognathus** (a tapir). **Inia** (a dolphin, upper part of Amazon basin). Six p.g. of *Muridæ ;* six p.g. of *Octodontidæ* (rat-like forms), two of them peculiar to W. Indies ; eight p.g. of *Echimyidæ*

(spiny rats) ; two p.g. of *Cercolabidæ* (tree porcupines). **Solenodon** (a hedgehog-like form from Cuba and Hayti). Twenty-six p.g. of bats, including the Vampires. Five p.g. of *Canidæ;* three p.g. of *Mustelidæ;* **Nasua** (coati) and **Cercoleptes** (Kinkajou) ; **Tremarctos** (spectacled bear) ; **Otaria** (an eared seal).

Peculiar Species.—Among these are, twenty species of **Didelphys** (to which genus most opossums belong). The American tapir. A species of racoon (genus **Procyon**).

Absent Forms.—*Ungulata* are scarce, deer and llamas being the only ruminants, tapirs and peccaries the only non-ruminants. The only insectivores are **Solenodon** and a species of shrew (**Sorex**). The *Viverridæ* are absent.

VI. *Nearctic Region.*—Thirty-two families are represented, of which one is peculiar, while one other is almost so, *i.e. Haploödontidæ* (rat-like forms allied to beavers and marmots), and *Saccomyidæ* (the pouched rats, of which one genus ranges into the N. of the Neotropical region).

Peculiar Genera (besides those in the above families).—**Antilocapra** (prong-horned antelope), **Aplocerus** (a goat-like antelope), and **Ovibos** (the musk-sheep). Three p.g. of *Muridæ,* **Jaculus** (a jerboa), **Cynomys** (the so-called prairie dog), and **Erethizon** (the tree porcupine), three p.g. of moles, two p.g. of bats, two p.g. of *Mustelidæ;* **Eumetopias** (an eared seal ; **Halicyon** (a seal).

Peculiar Species.—Among these are two of **Didelphys**, a peccary, several deer, the American bison, racoons, and the grizzly bear (**Ursus ferox**).

Absent Forms.—Ungulates are ill represented, deer, the American bison, two antelopes, a sheep, and the musk-sheep, being the only ruminants, while a peccary (Texas to Red River), is the only non-ruminant. Hedgehogs, *Viverridæ,* and monkeys are all unrepresented.

Distribution of Orders—

1. *Monotremata.*—Consists of only three genera, limited to part of the Australian region. *See* p. 188.

No fossil forms are found elsewhere, so that the place of origin of this order is unknown.

2. *Marsupialia.*—Consists of seven families (comprising thirty-six genera), of which only one, the Opossum family (including three genera), occurs outside the Australian region. The Opossums are Neotropical and Nearctic.

Fossil opossums occur in the Pleistocene of America, and in much older European deposits (Eocene to Miocene). The Secondary rocks of Europe contain a number of small forms, which probably resemble the ancestors of the Australian Marsupials. We may therefore suppose that this order originated in the Palæarctic region, and then extended into what is now Australia (at that time united by land with Asia), isolation occurring soon after, followed by specialization in various directions. The Opossums seem first to have existed in Europe, from whence they spread into America by former northerly land-connections.

3. *Edentata.*—This order is now chiefly limited to S. America, but **Orycteropus** is peculiar to the Ethiopian region, while **Manis** is found both in that and the Oriental region.

The geological evidence is in favour of considerable development in Africa, whence the order would spread north to the Oriental and Palæarctic regions, and thence on to America. The competition with higher forms has caused this extinction in most areas, and Edentates appear to be most abundant in S. America, because the competition with other animals is there comparatively small. The peculiar burrowing or climbing habits of most of the genera also tend to preserve them, and these habits no doubt represent attempts to escape from the severe competition with higher forms. The size of existing Edentates is insignificant compared with that of Pleistocene S. American and European genera.

4. *Ungulata.*—(a) Artiodactyla. *Non-rumniantia.* Swine are only represented in America by peccaries **(Dicotyles)**; true swine are found in all the other regions but only extend into the Australian as far as New Guinea. These animals are first known in the European Eocene, and during Miocene and Pliocene times were as common in N. America as Europe, but since then have almost entirely disappeared from the former area.

The hippopotamus is now limited to the Ethiopian region, but fossil forms occur in Europe (Pliocene and Pleistocene) and India (Miocene).

Ruminantia.—Recent *Camelidæ* are only found in the Neotropical and Palæarctic regions, but numerous forms occur in the Miocene and later deposits of N. America, where the group originated.

Tragulidæ or mouse-deer have also a discontinuous area of distribution—W. Africa **(Hyomoschus)** and Oriental region **(Tragulus)**. This is accounted for by the presence of Miocene forms in Europe, whence the family extended south.

Deer occur in all the regions except the Ethiopian, but do not extend far into the Australian region. They appear to have taken origin in the Old World, from whence they reached N. America in Miocene times, and afterwards passed to S. America.

Giraffes are at the present time confined to the Ethiopian region, but fossil forms are known from S. Europe and India, and a northern temperate origin is probable.

Bovidæ (oxen, sheep, antelopes, &c.) are present in all the regions except the Neotropical, though they only just pass into the Australian, and are scarce in the Nearctic. The family appears to have originated in the Palæarctic and Oriental regions during Miocene times.

(b) Perissodactyla. Tapirs present a striking example of discontinuous distribution, being found, on the one hand, in the Malay peninsula, Sumatra, and Borneo, and on the other, in S. and Central America. True tapirs occur in the W. of Europe as far back as Miocene times, but in America are not found further back than the Pleistocene. Migration from the Palæarctic region is thus indicated.

Rhinoceroses are now only Ethiopian and Oriental, but they appear to have originated in the Palæarctic region, where they extend back to the Miocene period. In Pliocene times they also ranged into N. America.

The genus **Equus** (horse, ass, zebra) is now limited to the Ethiopian and Palæarctic regions. It appears to have originated in the latter area during Miocene times, and then migrated not only into the Ethiopian, but also into the Oriental, Nearctic, and Neotropical regions, as proved by fossil forms.

5. *Sirenia.*—*See* p. 203.

6. *Rodentia.*—Very widely distributed ; occurring in all the regions, but in Madagascar and Australia only represented by *Muridæ*. They attain their largest development in S. America.

The order is of great geological antiquity, for some living genera extend back to the Eocene. Rodents probably originated in the Palæarctic region, whence migrations took place at an early date to S. America and S. Africa, allowing time for great specialization.

7. *Proboscidea.*—Elephants are now limited to the Ethiopian and Oriental regions, but formerly had a much wider extension.

Palæarctic forms occur from Miocene to Pleistocene times, and elephants have lived in India since the Miocene period. Numerous fossil examples occur in the Pliocene and Pleistocene deposits of N. and S. America.

8. *Hyracoidea.*—Almost entirely limited to the Ethiopian region, but range northwards as far as Syria.

9. *Insectivora.*—Very widely distributed, and represented by numerous specialized forms. Absent from S. America and Australia.

This order is a very ancient one, as shown by the fact that Miocene forms mostly belong to existing families. Extinction appears to be slowly taking place, and has led to many cases of discontinuous distribution, *e.g.*, the *Centetidæ*, represented by **Solenodon** in the W. Indies, and **Centetes**, with four other genera, in Madagascar.

10. *Cheiroptera.*—Bats, as might be expected, are found in all the great areas, but the Frugivora are absent from the Nearctic and Neotropical regions, as are the Horse-shoe bats (*Rhinolophidæ*) among insectivorous forms. On the other hand, the Leaf-nosed bats (*Phyllostomidæ*) are almost exclusively Neotropical.

Fossil bats, very like recent species, date from Eocene times, and the order is undoubtedly one of extreme antiquity.

11. *Carnivora.*—(a) Fissipedia. Occur in all the regions, except, perhaps, the Australian (the "native dog" of Australia is only doubtfully indigenous), but are especially characteristic of the Ethiopian and Oriental, which possess almost all the *Viverridæ* and *Hyænidæ*, with a great many of the *Felidæ* and *Mustelidæ*. Two genera, **Cryptoprocta** and **Proteles**, constituting distinct families, are limited respectively to Madagascar and S. Africa. Bears, however, are absent from the Ethiopian region, and are only represented by one species in the Neotropical region, which is also very poor in other Carnivora. The *Procyonidæ* are small bear-like forms, found in the Nearctic and Neotropical regions, and include the racoons (**Procyon**), coatis (**Nasua**), and kinkajous (**Cercoleptes**).

Fossil Carnivores date back to the Lower Eocene, but the recent families were not then differentiated. The order appears to have originated in the northern half of the Old World.

(b) Pinnipedia.—Seals are limited to cold and temperate seas, and are also found in the Caspian, Sea of Aral, and Lake Baikal, all of which, at no very distant epoch, were connected with the Arctic Ocean.

Walruses characterise the North Polar regions.

12. *Prosimiæ.*—(a) Cheiromyini. Only one form, the aye-aye (**Cheiromys**) which is restricted to Madagascar.

(b) Lemurini.—Practically limited to the Ethiopian and Oriental regions. **Indris**, **Lemur**, and four other genera are only found in Madagascar. **Tarsius** constitutes a distinct family, and is limited to Sumatra, Banca, Borneo, and Celebes.

Lemurs date back to the Eocene in Europe.

13. *Primates.*—(a) Arctopitheci and (b) Platyrrhini are confined to the Neotropical region.

(c) Catarrhini are found only in the Old World.

C y n o m o r p h a are especially Ethiopian and Oriental, but also extend into the Palæarctic region, and into the Australian region as far as Timor.

A n t h r o p o m o r p h a present a marked example of discontinuous distribution. *See* p. 222.

The order dates back to the Eocene.

Origin and Migrations of the Mammalia.

—The Class, and most likely all the Orders, originated in the Northern Hemisphere. Australia was isolated at a very early date, and therefore has preserved a very ancient Mammalian fauna. S. America and S. Africa were severed somewhat later, to be afterwards re-united, and they also have preserved some very ancient forms. The northerly connection between the Eastern and Western Hemispheres was then broken, not only by submergence of land, but also by a lowering of temperature. The Oriental and Ethiopian regions were also marked off by the formation of the Himalayas and the desert zone stretching from the Sahara to Central Asia.

GEOLOGICAL RANGE OF THE CHIEF ANIMAL GROUPS

Column headings (animal groups): Foraminifera. Radiolaria. Porifera. Hydrozoa. Anthozoa. Chætopoda. Crinoidea. Asterida. Ophiurida. Echinoidea. Holothuroidea. Crustacea. Arachnida Branchiata. Arachnida Tracheata. Myriapoda. Insecta. Polyzoa. Brachiopoda. All the Classes of Mollusca.

Age.	Formation.
CAINOZOIC OR TERTIARY.	Recent.
	Pleistocene.
	Pliocene.
	Miocene.
	Oligocene.
	Eocene.
MESOZOIC OR SECONDARY.	Cretaceous.
	Jurassic { Oolite. Lias.
	Trias.
PALÆOZOIC OR PRIMARY.	Dyas (Permian).
	Carboniferous.
	Devonian or Old Red Sandstone.
	Silurian.
	Ordovician.
	Cambrian.
ARCHÆAN.	Precambrian.

Printed in Great Britain
by Amazon

26589205R00145